Children's Church Specials

Group

Loveland, Colorado

CHILDREN'S CHURCH SPECIALS

Credits

Contributing Authors: E. Paul Allen, Mike Gillespie, Elaine Friedrich Hall, Cindy Hansen, Bob Latchaw, Karl and Gina Leuthauser, Julie Meiklejohn, Amy Nappa, Lori Haynes Niles, and Joclyn Wampler
Book Acquisitions Editor: Beth Rowland Wolf
Editor: Ivy Beckwith
Chief Creative Officer: Joani Schultz
Art Director: Jean Bruns
Cover Art Director: Jeff A. Storm
Cover Designer: Elise Lansdon
Computer Graphic Artist: Joyce Douglas
Illustrator: Kate Flanagan
Production Manager: Peggy Naylor

Library of Congress Cataloging-in-Publication Data
Children's church specials.
     p.   cm.
   ISBN 0-7644-2063-1 (alk. paper)
   1. Worship (Religious education)   I. Group Publishing.
BV1522.C48   1998
264' .0083--dc21   98-15018
                                   CIP

10 9 8 7   07 06 05
Printed in the United States of America.

Visit our Web site: **www.group.com**

Contents

Our Special God

Special Days

Introduction

People who work with children want the children to participate in and understand worship, but no one is really sure how to do it. How do we make children's worship different from Sunday school? How can we teach the kids to actively reflect on the character of God? *Children's Church Specials* can begin to lead your kids in truly understanding God, acts of worship, and why we worship.

Each worship session is built around a specific characteristic of God's. Kids learn about this one characteristic and what it means to us that God is like this. They actively praise God for being who he is and participate in activities that help them reflect on the characteristic of God's. Plus several of the worship sessions are tied to special holidays we all celebrate.

Each worship session contains "Praise," "Point," and "Prayer" sections. During the "Praise" time, kids praise God and participate in songs, games, prayers, and other activities that introduce kids to one characteristic of God's. Active-learning experiences in the "Point" section thoroughly engage kids, so they'll remember the point long after the session is over. The last section is "Prayer." There kids again thank God for being who he is because of the particular characteristic. Kids also look toward what this knowledge about God means for their own lives. Finally, children ask for God's help in the coming weeks to incorporate what they've learned into their own lives.

Each worship session ends with a "Time Stretcher." These are activities to help you when you anticipate needing a longer worship service than usual. If your church's worship service always runs longer than an hour, you may want to plan to use the "Time Stretcher" every week. "Time Stretcher" supplies are not included in the supplies list for each worship session, so be sure to check the activity for the supplies you'll need.

We suggest worship and praise songs to use as part of each worship session. Some are old, familiar hymns, while others may be new songs to you. Any song not readily available in a hymnal is taken from *Group's Singable Songs for Children's Ministry* (Group Publishing, Inc., 1996). You may purchase the accompaniment and leaders guide, the corresponding four volumes of cassettes or compact discs, and the two corresponding Lyrics Big Books at your local Christian bookstore. We've indicated in an index on which volume of cassette or CD the song appears. We've also indicated whether the song is included in one of the Lyrics Big Books. You may also substitute other songs or your own versions of the suggested songs. Please feel free to add more songs to each session if your children like to sing a lot.

Group sizes for children's worship vary from church to church. These sessions are written for small- to medium-size groups, but we've included tips so you can adapt activities for larger groups.

These worship sessions include lively activities for active kids. At the beginning of each session, establish an attention-getting signal with your children. For example, ringing a bell or turning the lights on and off are simple signals that tell children it's time to pay attention to you.

We hope you find *Children's Church Specials* helpful as you teach children how to worship and praise our great God.

Working With Combined Age Levels

We've designed *Children's Church Specials* so all age levels can learn about God and worship on an equal basis. Every worship session includes tips for incorporating kids of all ages into the activities.

But there are some things to remember about working with combined age levels in a large group setting. Strive for a balance of ages in small groups because the older kids can help the younger ones. If an activity calls for reading and writing skills, pair a reader with a non-reader. When you teach songs, be sure to repeat the words to the songs with the kids before they sing. Don't assume everyone in your group can read the words. Don't be concerned that discussions may be too difficult for younger kids to understand. Usually they'll be able to keep up. If you make the sessions too simple, you'll lose the older kids.

You'll find tips for using these sessions with combined age levels throughout the sessions. Because of the active-learning techniques used in each lesson, you'll be able to capture each child's attention and keep it during the entire session.

Relax, and enjoy the contributions children of all ages make to these worship sessions.

Our

· · · · ·

Special

· · · · ·

God

God Is All-Knowing

HOW TO USE THIS WORSHIP SESSION

Use this session any time your kids are facing a new beginning—at the beginning of the calendar year or the school year, for example.

OBJECTIVES

Kids will
- celebrate a new beginning,
- learn about the security of God's all-knowing love and presence, and
- decide specific ways they want God to help them this year.

YOU'LL NEED

- a Bible
- decorating supplies including party hats, party horns, confetti, construction paper, markers, and masking tape
  - scissors
  - photocopies of the "God's Promises" handout (p. 16)
  - a 9- or 11-inch balloon for each child
  - several large trash bags
  - self-stick notes
  - pencils
  - a large container, such as a trash can or plastic tub, for balloons
  - a sign that reads, "Wishing Well"
  - a pin
  - a sign that reads, "God's Promises"
  - a long rope for a game of Tug of War
  - white paper plates
  - *Group's Singable Songs for Children's Ministry* (See index on pp. 121-122.)

THE POINT

God knows the future.

TEACHER TIP

If you don't want to use confetti, use strips of crepe paper as streamers instead.

BIBLE BASIS

Matthew 6:25-34; 19:26; and John 14:27

The start of anything new brings new hopes and dreams. It's like a deep, cleansing breath followed by a sigh. What came before is gone, never to return again. With it went joys and sorrows. Now comes a new beginning. What will it hold?

Jesus knew life was difficult and full of worry. He watched as people lived from day to day, just getting by. Just making enough money to buy food. Just having the bare necessities of shelter. Just owning a few articles of clothing. Jesus knew that the knowledge of God's hope and love for each person was often lost in the daily struggle for survival. Worry had a way of taking the joy out of living.

In his Sermon on the Mount, Jesus tells us to stop worrying (Matthew 6:25-34). He wants us to place absolute trust in God's providential care and seek God's kingdom first. If we will, our lives will enter a new realm of peace and joy.

Again, later in his ministry, Jesus sounds the trumpet of assurance when he tells us, "With God all things are possible" (Matthew 19:26).

Children need to hear and believe that message. They need to know that God is watching over them at all times. God knows what their dreams and hopes are for new beginnings. God is with them as they work hard to achieve something important. God knows when they fail or when their dreams don't come true. At the start of something new, children can feel secure because God's presence is more powerful than any worry or disappointment.

The journey of faith—even for a child—means accepting the truth of Jesus as an absolute. When we read that Jesus said to his disciples, "Peace I leave with you; my peace I give you" (John 14:27), we know it's also meant for us and for the children we love. A new beginning is a time to celebrate; it's a time to experience God's peaceful presence and the security that comes from understanding that God knows the future.

UNDERSTANDING YOUR KIDS

A new beginning—whether it be a new calendar year or a new school year—can be an exciting time for kids. They have a chance to dream about the future. This is particularly important for a child who has faced a tragedy, disappointment, or another setback the previous year.

During this session, be sensitive to children who are bringing hurt feelings to your celebration of a new beginning. Assure them of God's all-knowing love. The new adventure holds many opportunities for them. Encourage them to trust in God's care as Jesus taught us in the Sermon on the Mount.

Other children will enter the new beginning with everything

going for them. But they, too, need to connect with God. Even if great things have happened to these children in the past several months, it's easy for them to forget that God was present during those victories.

Yes, it's a new beginning, and God is starting it with us. That's good news for your kids. God knows they're secure in his loving arms. No matter what happens in the coming year, God's grace is sufficient.

PRAISE

Celebrate What's New!

Before the session, set up a table in the center of your meeting area, and put the decorating supplies on it. Give two or three adult volunteers party hats, party horns, and confetti. Have adults hide in or nearby the room so the children can't see the adults. Tell adults that toward the beginning of the session, you'll say, "Happy New Year's to all of you" to the children. Explain that at that point, the adults should come out of hiding; blow their horns; throw their confetti; and say, "Happy New Year's!"

Welcome the children, and ask them to sit in a group. Ask:

● **What are some things that are new to us every year?**

After kids have responded with answers such as "a new school," "a new class," and "a new teacher," say: **One of the things that is new every year is the year itself, and people like to celebrate that new beginning. Even if it's not New Year's right now, we can celebrate the new things we're starting with a New Year's celebration. So happy New Year's to all of you!** Step back as the adult volunteers come out of hiding; blow their horns; throw their confetti; and say, "Happy New Year's!" Say: **Now that we've started all this excitement, let's decorate our meeting area for a New Year's party. Find a partner, go to the decorations table, and decide how you want to help decorate. You can hang streamers, make a "Happy New Year's" sign, or make something special for everyone to wear. You have five minutes to make your decorations and decorate the room.** Ask adult volunteers to help the pairs decorate.

After five minutes, have everyone sit in a circle. Say: **You did a fantastic job decorating for our New Year's celebration. Let's start our party by singing "This Is the Day" (Group's Singable Songs for Children's Ministry).** Each time children sing the word "day," have them jump up and quickly sit back down. Have children sing through the song twice so everyone knows the words.

Say: **Let's change this song into a New Year's song. When you come to the word "day," replace it with the words "new start."** Sing through the song once. Say: **Now when you say, "New start," jump**

TEACHER TIP

If you want to simplify this process, ask partners to use the decorating supplies to make party hats for each other. While kids are making hats, have the adults hang streamers.

If you have a very large group of children, set up various stations around the room for making decorations. Ask adult helpers to supervise those stations.

up and sing the words really loudly, but don't shout them. Before kids sing the song again, ask them to suggest a replacement for the word "day" that tells about the new year—the word "month" or "time," for example.

Say: **Our New Year's celebration is going great. Let's stop here and thank God for being with us. God knows everything that will happen when we find ourselves in new situations. Let's thank God for our new beginnings and for the opportunity we have to learn lots of good new things about the special plans God has for us. Let's thank God for taking care of us.** Say a prayer, thanking God for new beginnings.

POINT

Wishes for a New Beginning

Before the session, cut apart the verses from the "God's Promises" handouts (p. 16). Insert one verse into each uninflated balloon, and then blow up the balloons. Be sure to have one balloon for each child. Put the balloons into the large trash bags, and give each of the adult helpers a trash bag. Also tape the "Wishing Well" sign onto the large container.

Say: **Many people start something new by making a list of things they hope will happen. Sometimes we call this a list of resolutions. I wonder what some of your hopes and dreams are. Maybe you want to grow taller or do better in math. Maybe you want to play the piano better. We all hope good things will happen this year.**

I'm going to give each of you three self-stick notes and a pencil. On each note, write or draw one thing you hope will happen this year. I want the older children to help the younger children who can't write. When you finish your notes, bring them to one of the adults; the adult will put your notes on a balloon and give the balloon to you. Let's imagine that those balloons are going to be sailing high into the air and taking our hopes to God. When three notes are stuck on a balloon, the adult should give the balloon to the child who brought the notes. Ask kids to sit together and hold their balloons without bouncing them around.

When everyone has finished, ask children to share the hopes they wrote on the notes. Place the large container labeled "Wishing Well" in the middle of the group. Say: **You have some wonderful dreams for this year. I want each of you to put your balloon in the wishing well.**

When all the balloons are in the wishing well, say the following words as you reach into the wishing well and pop the balloons with a pin, one at a time. Say: **Sometimes we wish for things that don't**

TEACHER TIP

If you have a large group of children, make sure you have enough adults and balloons so kids can move through the first part of the activity quickly. Then treat the second part of the activity as an object lesson: Gather kids back into the large group, pop the balloons, and draw attention to the slips of paper. Ask several older kids to read aloud what the slips of paper say. Demonstrate sticking the "hopes" notes onto "God's promises," and continue with the activity as written.

come true [pop]. **We might wish we could play soccer better, but we don't** [pop]. **We might wish that the person who keeps picking on us will move away, but he doesn't** [pop]. **We might wish for a new bike, but we don't get one** [pop]. **We might wish we could play the piano better, but we don't play better** [pop]. Make up other wishes that apply to your group.

When you've popped all the balloons, show the wishing well containing the popped balloons to the kids. Ask:

- **How do you feel right now?**

- **What happened to all your wishes for the year?**

- **How is that like what sometimes happens to your hopes and dreams during the year?**

Dump out the container onto the floor. Ask kids what they see. When a child mentions the slips of paper, ask children to pick up the slips of paper and read them out loud one at a time.

Say: **Wow! What a surprise! All your balloons with your hopes on them were broken. But there was something inside the balloons you didn't know about. What's on those slips of paper you just read?** Allow time for kids to answer. Say: **Let's stick the self-stick notes onto the slips of paper.** Allow time for kids to do this. Say: **Watch what I do. I'm going to change the wishing well sign to a sign that says, "God's Promises." Now let's put all your hopes into the "new" container.**

Read Matthew 19:26 to the group. Ask:

- **What does Jesus mean by saying, "With God all things are possible"?**

Read aloud John 14:27. Ask:

- **What does Jesus mean by promising us his peace?**

Say: **Here's the kicker. God doesn't promise that everything we wish for will come true. But he does know what will happen in the future, and God promises he will always be with us no matter what happens. Sometimes our dreams do come true, and God wants that for us. Sometimes our dreams don't come true, but God is still there and wants to be with us when we're disappointed or hurt or mad. God's promises are not like a wishing well. God will love us and be with us every day.**

That's Not Fair

Have children form two teams, making sure one team has a few bigger kids on it than the other team—just enough so one team will have an advantage in a game of Tug of War. If some of the kids start complaining, encourage them to do their best. If you have more kids than team members, have the kids who watch cheer the teams on. Place a long rope on the floor, and mark a center area. Tell each team to grab one end of the rope. When you say "go," have kids start pulling. The team with the bigger kids should win. Have kids play again with the same teams.

After kids have played twice, ask:

- **What did you like about that game?**
- **What was unfair about that game?**
- **How was the game similar to what sometimes happens to your hopes and dreams?**
- **What do you want to say to God sometimes when things don't go your way?**

Collect the rope, and say: **One day a large crowd gathered to hear Jesus talk. He said lots of things that day to the crowd. One of the things he said can help us a lot when we start worrying about our dreams not coming true. Here's what he told that crowd. And I bet there were children there listening to him, too.**

Read aloud Matthew 6:25-34. Ask:

- **Why does Jesus say we don't need to worry about anything?**

Say: **Our game of Tug of War wasn't a fair game. In the coming year, sometimes your hopes and dreams won't come true. It won't be fair, just as our game wasn't fair. You might want to start worrying, but Jesus says that's not the answer. He wants us to remember that God knows what's best for us. Jesus wants us to stay close to him—even when we get really disappointed as some of you are now because the teams weren't fair. Something this year will happen to you that won't be fair. But Jesus will be there waiting to hold you. That's something I'm sure of.**

PRAYER

Paper Plate Promises

Have kids form multi-age groups of five. Give a marker and paper plate to each child. If you have a very large group of children, make sure you have enough adults to supervise the groups.

Say: **One way we can remember God's promises and plans this year is by talking to God in prayer. What is a short prayer you could write that would keep you close to God and his plans this year? You could say, "Dear God, Thank you for loving me so much. Thank you for sending Jesus to be with me. Thank you that you know what will happen in the future and that your promises always come true. I love you." Or you might write, "Dear God, I know you love me a lot. I know you're always with me through Jesus. I know you're there every day for me and you know what will happen tomorrow. Thank you."**

After you decide on your prayer, write or draw it on the paper plate. The older kids will help the younger ones with their prayers. Then help each other decorate the rim of the plates with

the markers. **You can take your prayer home and use it every day this year.**

When the groups finish working, ask volunteers to share their prayers with the whole group. The older kids can help the younger ones. After kids have shared, lead them in the following litany prayer. First teach kids to say, "God, you are always with us, and you know what will happen tomorrow." Have kids practice the sentence so they can repeat it after each of the leader's lines.

LEADER: **Dear God, thank you for new beginnings.**
CHILDREN: God, you are always with us, and you know what will happen tomorrow.
LEADER: **Thank you for helping us work hard to make our hopes and dreams come true.**
CHILDREN: God, you are always with us, and you know what will happen tomorrow.
LEADER: **Thank you for sending Jesus to teach us how much you love us.**
CHILDREN: God, you are always with us, and you know what will happen tomorrow.
LEADER: **Thank you for being with us every day of the year, even when things go wrong.**
CHILDREN: God, you are always with us, and you know what will happen tomorrow.
LEADER: **Thank you for making us your children.**
CHILDREN: God, you are always with us, and you know what will happen tomorrow.
LEADER: **Amen.**

TIME STRETCHER

New Year's Cards

Provide construction paper, scissors, markers, glue sticks, and the "God's Promises" verses kids used earlier (be sure to remove any self-stick notes from the verses). Tell children to get back with their partners from the beginning of the session. Ask partners to work together to make special "God's Promise" cards for their parents. On the outside of the construction paper cards, kids should write, "God's Promise." Inside the cards, kids should write one of the special "God's Promises" verses. Children who aren't able to write should glue verses into their cards.

God's Promises

*Prior to the worship session, copy this page, cut out each verse,
and insert one verse into each uninflated balloon. You'll need one balloon for each child.*

"For nothing is impossible with God" *(Luke 1:37).*

"Therefore, if anyone is in Christ, he is a new creation; the old has gone, the new has come" *(2 Corinthians 5:17).*

"For God so loved the world that he gave his one and only Son, that whoever believes in him shall not perish but have eternal life" *(John 3:16).*

"But the fruit of the Spirit is love, joy, peace, patience, kindness, goodness, faithfulness, gentleness, and self-control. Against such things there is no law" *(Galatians 5:22-23).*

"To the Jews who had believed him, Jesus said, 'If you hold to my teaching, you are really my disciples. Then you will know the truth, and the truth will set you free" *(John 8:31-32).*

"Do not be anxious about anything, but in everything, by prayer and petition, with thanksgiving, present your requests to God" *(Philippians 4:6).*

"And we know that in all things God works for the good of those who love him, who have been called according to his purpose" *(Romans 8:28).*

"This is the message we have heard from him and declare to you: God is light; in him there is no darkness at all" *(1 John 1:5).*

God Is Loving

HOW TO USE THIS WORSHIP SESSION

Use this session when you want to teach children about God's love or around Valentine's Day.

OBJECTIVES

Kids will
- discover ways God shows love,
- tell God they love him, and
- find ways to show others their love and God's love.

YOU'LL NEED

- a Bible
- crayons or markers
- newsprint
- masking tape
- pencils
- index cards
- a decorated valentine box that is labeled "God's Valentines"
- photocopies of the "Love Is..." handout (p. 23)
- for each child, a 1-foot length of red ribbon that's at least 2 inches wide
- black permanent markers
- a heart cut out of gold paper (patterns on p. 24) for each child
- a 1½-foot length of yarn for each child
- a hole punch
- fabric glue
- *Group's Singable Songs for Children's Ministry* (See index on pp. 121-122.)

BIBLE BASIS

1 Corinthians 13:4-8 and 1 John 4:7-12

Our world talks a lot about love, but the love expressed in songs and on greeting cards is nothing compared to the love God shows us through his Son, Jesus. We can help our students discover God's perfect love and celebrate it.

1 John 4:7-12 tells us true love comes from God. John says if a person doesn't love, he or she doesn't know God. And John tells us that God's love was made known to us through Jesus. Help your kids

THE POINT

God is loving.

understand the unconditional nature of God's love. It reaches far beyond the limits of human love.

Paul deals with love in 1 Corinthians 13:4-8. He emphasizes the importance of love in our lives and defines love.

Use this worship session to help your kids discover God's love by allowing their lives to overflow with it.

UNDERSTANDING YOUR KIDS

"What the world needs now is love, sweet love," are the beginning words of an old song. Today more than ever, our world needs love. Not the love the world gives, but the love of God.

Our kids are exposed to a variety of meanings for love, and few of them describe love as God sees it. Kids love their cats. Kids love a movie. Kids love a chocolate bar. But this understanding of love shows little experience of God's unconditional love for kids.

In this session, you have the opportunity to share God's love with your kids. Share how you've experienced God's love and how it affects your relationships with others. As you help kids discover God's perfect love, you can help them celebrate God's love in their own lives.

PRAISE

Love Praise

Welcome the kids, and then say: **Today we're going to talk about love. We're going to think about how much God loves us.** Lead kids in singing "Lord, I Lift Your Name on High" *(Group's Singable Songs for Children's Ministry)* several times. After you finish singing, ask:

● **What does this song tell us about God's love?**

● **According to this song, what should be our response to God's loving actions?**

Say: **Lots of things excite us. We get excited when our favorite sports team wins or when something special happens to us. Accepting God's love is like having something really special happen to us. We can be really excited about God loving us. Let's sing the song again and with our singing, show God how excited we are that he loves us.**

Love Prayer

After you finish singing, ask:

● **How many of you know that God loves you today?**

● **How has God shown love to you during the past week?** (You may need to follow up with questions such as "Did someone do a loving thing for you?" or "Did you see a beautiful sunset?" Examples will help kids understand how God shows love to us.)

Say: **We want to praise and thank God for showing love to us, so let's say a prayer together. I'll say, "Dear God, thank you for showing your love to me by..." and you can fill in the blank with a word or phrase describing some way God has shown love to you.** Start the prayer by thanking God for a way he's shown love to you, and then allow kids to complete the sentence as they like. After all who want to have prayed, ask:

● **How do people show that they love each other?**

Say: **In some of those same ways, God shows us that he loves us. He takes care of us. He gives us what we need. He watches over us and protects us. Let's sing a song about how God watches over us with his love.** Lead kids in singing "His Banner Over Me Is Love" *(Group's Singable Songs for Children's Ministry)* several times, and use the hand motions from the leaders guide or your own motions.

TEACHER TIP

If you have a large group of children, have them form smaller groups, and ask adult helpers to lead the smaller groups in this prayer.

God's Love Banners

After you finish singing, have kids form multi-age groups of four or five. Provide each group with a large piece of newsprint and crayons or markers. Say: **The song we just sang says God's love is like a banner. A banner is a hanging made out of paper or cloth that proclaims something. A "God's love" banner would tell anyone who looked at it about God's love. You're going to use the supplies I gave you to make banners that tell about God's love. First write on your newsprint in large letters, "God is love." Next use your imaginations to decorate your banner with pictures and other words that describe God's love. For example, you could draw a tree, food, friends, or family members.** Give groups several minutes to work on their banners. When they're finished, gather kids back together in a large group. Ask each group to show its banner and explain the pictures and words. Then display each banner around your meeting area. Have kids stand by the banners and sing "His Banner Over Me Is Love" one more time. Lead kids in a short prayer to thank God for loving us.

TEACHER TIP

If you use a meeting space in which it's difficult to hang the banners, have several of the older kids hold the banners high. Have the rest of the kids huddle under the banners to sing the song.

POINT

A Valentine for God

Say: **Valentine's Day is a special day when we tell other people we love them. One of the ways we do this is by giving each other cards or valentines.** Ask:

● **What are some ways you celebrate Valentine's Day?**

● **What special person would you like to send a valentine to?**

Give each child a pencil and a white index card. Say: **Today we're going to write a valentine to God. Decide what you would like to say or draw on your card. Do more than just sign your name. Write a message to God. Once you have finished your card, put it in the box labeled "God's Valentines" in the front of the room.** Have the older kids help the younger kids who can't write yet. When all the children have deposited their valentines in the box, ask:

● **Was it hard or easy to write a valentine to God? Why?**

● **How was writing a valentine to God different from writing a valentine to a person we can see? How was it the same?**

Say: **Just as it feels good when someone tells us we're loved, God likes it when we tell him we love him.** Ask:

What are some other ways we can show God we love him?

What the Bible Says About God's Love

Tape a blank piece of newsprint to a wall. Say: **The Bible has a lot to say about how much God loves us. We're going to read 1 John 4:7-12 to find out more about God's love.** Choose one of the older kids who is a good reader to stand and read aloud the passage to the group. Ask another child to be the "love recorder." Give that child a marker, and ask him or her to put a mark on the piece of newsprint every time the word "love" is read. Encourage the rest of the children to help by clapping their hands every time they hear the word "love." After the passage has been read, count the number of marks on the newsprint, and say: **Wow! Love was mentioned a lot in those Bible verses. Love must be really important to God. And because he loves us, he wants us to love other people.**

TEACHER TIP

If you use a meeting space that prohibits hanging things on the walls, use an overhead projector and a blank transparency for this activity.

Heart of Gold Medals

Before the session, cut apart the sentences from the "Love Is..." handout (p. 23). You'll need one sentence for every two children.

Have children form pairs that include an older child and a younger child. Give each pair one description of love from the handout, two pieces of red ribbon, a black permanent marker, two gold hearts, and two lengths of yarn. If you have more pairs than descriptions from the "Love Is..." handout, give some pairs duplicate descriptions. If you have fewer groups than descriptions from the "Love Is..." handout, choose several characteristics of love you want your group to focus on.

Say: **In the book of 1 Corinthians in the Bible, the Apostle Paul has a lot to say about love—especially about how we're supposed to love others because God loves us. Each pair has a phrase that describes some part of love as Paul wrote about it in 1 Corinthians 13. With your partner, read your phrase and talk about how**

this characteristic is part of love. **Then use the marker to write the phrase down the length of your ribbon. Then use a hole punch to punch a hole in the top of each gold heart. When you've done that, run your yarn through the hole, and knot the ends to make a necklace. Next glue the ribbon to the bottom of the gold heart. That's how you make "heart of gold" medals.** After kids have finished making their medals, collect them to use in a later activity.

PRAYER

God's Gold

Gather kids together in a large group. Say: **Today we've celebrated God's love for us. We've learned that because God loves us, he expects us to love other people. And we've talked about ways to show that love to other people. But we don't want to leave our good, loving thoughts here. We want to love people at home and love other people we meet because God loves us.**

Get the medals kids made in the previous activity, and have kids line up by the "God's love" banners they made earlier. Say: **I will award each of you a heart of gold medal to take home with you. Each medal talks about a way we can show love to others. Your job for this week is to live up to the word on your medal by showing love to other people.** Put a medal over each child's head as people do in award ceremonies. It's not important for the children to get the same medals they each made. As you award each medal, read aloud the description of love and add a sentence telling how the child could live out that kind of love during the week. For example, you might say, "Brent is awarded the 'love angers slowly' medal. When his little sister bothers him this week, he won't get angry at her as quickly."

After you've awarded all the medals, gather kids in a circle; then say: **Isn't it great that God loves us, takes care of us, and protects us? And God helps us to love others. Sometimes loving others is hard, but with God's help and your special medals, you'll be able to love others this week.** Close in prayer, thanking God for his love and asking for his help in loving other people during the week.

TIME STRETCHER

"God's Promises" Cards

Have available red and white construction paper, glue, glitter, markers, doilies, and other art supplies. Say: **Today we're celebrating God's love for us. Think about someone you love a lot. You're going to make a special card for that person. In the card, let that**

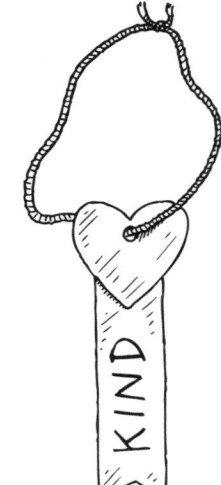

KIND

TEACHER TIP

If you have a large group of children, hold simultaneous, separate medal ceremonies for each age level. For example, send all the first-graders to one area of your meeting space, and have an adult helper award their medals; send the second-graders to a different area; and so on.

person know that God loves them and that you love them. You can decorate the card any way you want, but be sure to include a message of God's love. Have older kids help the younger kids with any writing. When kids are done, remind them to give the cards to the people they were thinking of.

Love Is...

Prior to the worship session, make photocopies of this page, and cut out each sentence.

Love is patient.	Love angers slowly.
Love is kind.	Love doesn't hold a grudge.
Love doesn't want what others have.	Love tells the truth.
Love doesn't brag.	Love protects others.
Love isn't proud.	Love trusts others.
Love is polite.	Love helps others be hopeful; love never gives up.
Love isn't selfish.	Love goes on forever.

Heart Patterns

Use these patterns to cut out a heart of gold paper for each child.

God Is Forgiving

HOW TO USE THIS WORSHIP SESSION

Use this session prior to Easter or any time you want your kids to reflect on God's forgiveness.

OBJECTIVES

Kids will
- explore the meaning and result of confession,
- have an opportunity to experience forgiveness, and
- celebrate our forgiving God.

YOU'LL NEED

- Bibles
- for every 6 to 8 children, an inexpensive welcome mat
- cups of gold sequins
- cups of bacon bits
- markers
- eye shadow
- baby wipes
- cookies, cupcakes, or other party treats
- napkins
- *Group's Singable Songs for Children's Ministry* (See index on pp. 121-122.)

BIBLE BASIS

Luke 15:11-24 and 1 John 1:9

The parable of the lost son in Luke 15:11-24 shows us what God's forgiveness is all about. After greedily grabbing all the goods his father had to offer and then coming up empty, the son sat down and thought about where his selfishness had gotten him. He saw he was in terrible need of forgiveness from his loving and compassionate father. The young man's restoration was complete when his father threw his arms around the son, celebrating that his son who was once dead was alive again!

Our celebration of God's forgiveness can follow the same path. In 1 John 1:9, we're assured that our loving God is faithful to forgive our sins when we recognize the need for forgiveness. God throws his arms around us in celebration of Jesus' resurrection, and our forgiveness is complete.

THE POINT

God forgives confessed sin.

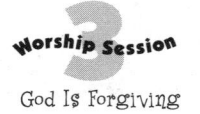
UNDERSTANDING YOUR KIDS

Some kids are naturally introspective. For others, looking inside is a learned skill, but an important one. Reflection about personal sin can be difficult for kids.

When younger kids think about their sin, they can slip into feelings of shame about being "bad" kids. Older kids tend to protect themselves from those feelings through denial. You can recognize this denial when kids make jokes and wisecracks about serious misbehavior. These feelings can lead kids to a detour on their faith journey if we don't show them which fork in the road God wants them to take.

As Christian teachers, we have the privilege of pointing children to the joy of forgiveness through honest confession. Kids need to know that their feelings of guilt can lead them directly to God's grace. God has no bad kids! Jesus died and rose again so that God's cleansing and restoring of his creation would be complete. This worship session should leave two words ringing in your kids' ears: Welcome home!

PRAISE

Forgiveness Praise

Have kids sing "Sing (If You Wanna Be Happy)" (*Group's Singable Songs for Children's Ministry*). After kids have finished singing, have them turn to a partner and tell one thing that has made them feel unhappy. After about one minute, say: **Raise your hand if you mentioned something you had done wrong.** Wait for kids to respond, and then say: **Raise your hand if you mentioned something someone else had done wrong.** Wait for kids to respond, and then ask:

● **What do you think brings back happiness after we've done something wrong or after someone has wronged us?**

Say: **In our time together today, we're going to talk about forgiveness and especially about how God is forgiving. God's forgiveness can give us a happy feeling!**

Sing part or all of the song again. Then have kids sing "He Forgives Me" (*Group's Singable Songs for Children's Ministry*).

Have kids turn to the same partner and describe to each other what they know about God's forgiveness. After kids have had a chance to share, say: **God forgives us when we tell him we're sorry for things we've done that make him sad. Then it's as if we never had done those things.**

POINT

A Son Who Was Forgiven

Have kids form multi-age groups of six to eight. Pass out one welcome mat to each group. Have the groups sit on the floor around their welcome mats. Give each group a Bible. Ask:

● **Why do homes often have welcome mats outside the front doors?**

Say: **I'd like for you to imagine that you're standing at the door of a wealthy man's home in biblical times. The story, which we can find in Luke 15:11-24, begins at this wealthy man's house. Let's have the person in your group who's the oldest find that story in the Bible and then place the open Bible on the welcome mat.**

To really understand this story, you have to know a couple of things about Jewish customs. The first is about inheritances. An inheritance is the money given to others when someone dies. In Jewish families, the oldest son got twice as much as any of his brothers. Since the father in our story was wealthy, he had a pretty full cup of riches. Give each group a cup of sequins. Say: **Put your cup of sequins on the welcome mat, and keep the sequins in your cup.**

The second thing you need to know is how Jewish families felt about pigs. God told Jewish people in their laws not to eat pork, and pigs were disgusting to them. Pass a cup of bacon bits to each group, and then say: **Put your cup of bacon bits in the center of your group—but not on the welcome mat because Jewish people wouldn't allow pork in their houses. Listen for directions about these two cups as I tell the story of the lost son.**

In the home where you now are gathered, a man lived with his two sons. One day the younger son came to his father and said, "Father, I want my inheritance now." Pass the cup of sequins around your group, and each of you take five sequins out of the cup. Return all the leftovers to the welcome mat because the older son didn't take his inheritance. It stayed with the father at their home.** Give kids time to follow your directions.

Say: **So you now have riches just as the younger son did. Listen closely as I continue the story. Each time something happens to the son that you think made the father sad, I want you each to put one sequin in the cup with the bacon bits and take one bacon bit out of the cup.**

The son gathered all his things together and set off for a distant land. Pause.

He wasted all his money in wild living and partying. Pause.

He spent all the money he had. Pause.

Then there was no food where the son lived. He was in trouble because he didn't have any food or money. Pause.

He went to work for a citizen of that country, and the citizen

TEACHER TIP

If welcome mats won't work for your situation, use poster board and markers. You might want to provide a model so kids can copy the letters of the word "welcome" onto their "mat" before you start the story.

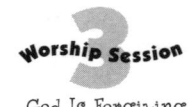
sent him out to the fields to feed the pigs. Pause.

The son was so hungry that he wanted to eat what the pigs were eating, but no one gave him anything. Pause.

The son sat down and looked in his hands. Look in your hands and tell your group what you think the younger son might have said to himself. Pause to allow kids to discuss this.

Say: **The Bible tells us that when the son came to his senses, he said, "My father's hired men have food to spare, and here I am with pigs, starving to death. I'm going home! I'll tell my father that I know I have sinned against God and against him. I'm not worthy to be his son anymore, but maybe I can work for him." So the son left the pigs.**

Put the bacon bits back into the cup, and leave them there just as the son left the pigs in the far-off land. Ask:

● **How do you think the son felt as he traveled home?**

● **Smell your hands. What does the smell remind you of from the story?**

Say: **The father saw his son coming home while he was still a long way off, and he knew his son realized he'd been wrong. His son showed this by coming home. He felt very sorry for his son. He ran to his son and threw his arms around him and kissed him.**

The son said, "Father, I'm so sorry. I let God down, and I let you down. Just let me come back and work for you. I don't expect to be treated as a son anymore."

As you tell the next part of the story, walk around to each group and take some of the sequins from each cup. Toss the sequins into the air around the children like confetti as you describe the things the father told his servants to do.

Say: **The father began yelling at his servants, saying, "Quick! Bring the best robe, and put it on my son! Hurry! Put a ring on his finger! Get moving! Get the boy some sandals! Run to the field! Kill the best calf so we can have a barbecue! We're going to have a party! My son was lost, but now he's come home!"** Ask:

● **Why do you think the father acted that way?**

● **How do you think the son felt?**

● **What do you think would have happened if the son had not come home?**

● **What do you think would have happened if the son had come home but had never apologized?**

Pass out the markers, and encourage the kids to decorate their mats with celebration designs. While decorating their mats, ask kids to discuss the following questions:

● **Think about a time you had to apologize. How did you feel?**

● **Think about a time you were forgiven. What happened?**

Use the mats at the door of your church or doors of individual classrooms.

PRAYER

Confession Session

Play this version of the game Simon Says, giving the verbal instructions but occasionally throwing in a visual clue that will mislead all but the most attentive kids. For example, say, "Simon says, 'Touch your nose' " while pointing to your ear. Instead of calling kids "out" when they don't follow the verbal directions correctly, put a mark of eye shadow somewhere on their skin. Play until everyone has at least one spot of eye shadow.

Then have kids choose a partner. Give each pair a baby wipe. Say: **Starting with the partner who is wearing the most white, I would like each of you to point to your dark spots one at a time and tell your partner what you did wrong in the game to get that spot. As you remember each mistake, your partner will use the baby wipe to clean off the dark spot.** Give the kids several minutes to complete the activity, and then have them sit in a large circle.

Say: **What you just did is called confession. You thought about your mistakes and confessed them to your partner. Some of you may have had a hard time remembering what each mistake was. Confession is an important part of prayer. We can go to God and ask him to wipe us clean of all the wrong things we've done. Once we've been wiped clean, those dark spots are gone forever.** Open a Bible to Psalm 130:3-4, and say: **The Bible says, "If you, O Lord, kept a record of sins, O Lord, who could stand? But with you there is forgiveness." God forgives us when we confess our sins to him.**

Say: **Now we're going to take a little quiet time to think about some of the things we've done that make God sad. We need to understand when we have done wrong things.** Open a Bible to 1 John 1:9. **The Bible says that if we're honest, we have to admit we've sinned. If we confess our sins, God is faithful and just and will forgive our sins and make us as if we never had sinned. We don't have to confess to everybody what we've done wrong—just to God. So I'm going to ask that you not talk to your friends while you're thinking. When you think of something you've done wrong, tell God about it and then ask him to forgive you. God never forces people to confess their sins, so if you don't want to participate in this activity, you don't have to. Just sit quietly and wait until everyone finishes.**

Pray together: **Thank you, heavenly Father, for the children who have spoken to you today. Now bless our time of celebrating your forgiveness. Amen.** Serve cookies, cupcakes, or other party treats, and celebrate God's forgiveness together.

TEACHER TIP

If you have a large group of kids, have them form groups of ten to twelve for the game of Simon Says. Each group will need some eye shadow. Have adult volunteers lead each group in the game. After the game is complete and each child has received a mark of eye shadow, gather the whole group back together.

TEACHER TIP

If you're using this lesson at Easter and your church observes the Lenten season, this is an appropriate time to explain the preparations your church is making.

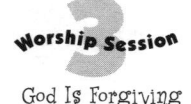

TIME STRETCHERS

Wrinkle Remover

For this activity, you'll need squares of tissue paper, an iron, and a safe place to cool the iron. Give each child a piece of tissue paper. Have children crumple their pieces of tissue paper and then try to straighten the pieces out again. Ask how the tissue paper is like our lives. Brainstorm for ways to restore the paper. Carefully iron the paper to remove the wrinkles. Cool the iron safely out of the children's way.

Lenten Decoration

Provide a purple scarf or length of fabric and glitter glue or glittery fabric paint. Let the kids put a symbol of their forgiveness on the fabric with the glitter glue or paint. Drape the finished scarf over a cross or hang it above the door of your worship area until Easter.

God Is Creator

HOW TO USE THIS WORSHIP SESSION

Use this session to celebrate all the birthdays of the kids in your group. Use it, also, to help kids reflect on God's role as creator.

OBJECTIVES

Kids will
- discover that they have many unique qualities and
- have a birthday party to celebrate that God created each of them special.

YOU'LL NEED

- a Bible
- ink pads
- markers
- a 2-foot-long piece of newsprint for each child
- a chalkboard and chalk or a dry-erase board and a marker
- a 4-foot-long piece of butcher paper for each child
- scissors
- tape
- slips of paper
- pens or pencils
- a hole punch
- ribbon
- lollipops
- photocopies of the "God Made Me Special" handout (p. 36)
- undecorated cupcakes
- bowls of frosting
- plastic knives
- sprinkles or other decorations
- napkins
- *Group's Singable Songs for Children's Ministry* (See index on pp. 121-122.)

BIBLE BASIS

Psalm 139:13-16

A birthday is a special time to recognize and celebrate an individual's special and unique qualities, as well as acknowledge the

THE POINT

God made each of us special.

TEACHER TIP

This worship session simulates a birthday party. For added fun and an element of surprise, you may want to decorate your meeting area ahead of time. Be as simple or as elaborate as time and space allow.

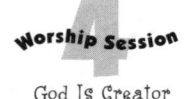

creativity of our creator, God.

God created everything in our world. The uniqueness of each human being is a tribute to God's unlimited creativity. And Psalm 139 demonstrates clearly and beautifully not only that God put into motion his perfect plan when he created each one of us, but also that God continues to be intimately involved in our daily lives. This knowledge is truly cause for celebration.

UNDERSTANDING YOUR KIDS

The idea of each person being special and unique is, generally, an easy one for kids to grasp. Many kids are capable of naturally accepting and even celebrating differences—more so than adults.

In this session, you'll help kids see that differences in people are all part of God's wonderful plan. You'll show them that we do, indeed, have many reasons to celebrate because God created each of us to be special.

PRAISE

Birthday Praise

Have kids sing "The Butterfly Song" (*Group's Singable Songs for Children's Ministry*) together. Then say: **We're having a birthday party today. This is a birthday party for each of you. We're celebrating the fact that God made each of us special. To start, I'll read a part of the Bible that tells us about the special way God created us.** Read aloud Psalm 139:13-16. Say: **This passage tells us God loved us and had a plan for us before we were even born. The passage also says we're "wonderfully made."** Ask:

● **What things about yourself do you think were wonderfully made? For example, God gave us fingers so we can write and pick up things.**

● **How do you think God wants us to feel about the special care he took in creating us?**

Say: **God wants us to praise him and tell him how thankful we are every time we think about these wonderful plans for us and how special God made us. One of the ways we can praise God is by having a party. One thing everybody needs at a birthday party is a party hat. You're going to make party hats now that you'll use later in our worship session. You'll write on the hats part of the Bible passage I just read to remind you that God made you special.**

To make your party hat special, just like you, use the ink pads to put your fingerprints on your hat. Then you can decorate your hat in your own way using the markers. Direct kids to tables or areas of your meeting space, and set out the supplies. Give

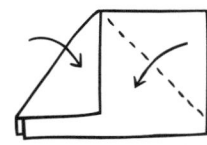
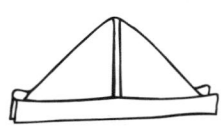

each child a piece of newsprint, and have kids decorate their hats using the ink pads and the markers. Write the words of Psalm 139:14 on a chalkboard, dry-erase board, or piece of newsprint, and have kids copy it onto their hats. Have older kids help younger kids. If you have a lot of nonwriters in your group, write out the passage ahead of time on small pieces of paper; then have kids glue the pieces of paper to their hats. Show kids how to fold their newsprint into hats using the pattern in the margin. You may want to make a hat ahead of time to show kids what the finished hats will look like.

After kids finish making their hats, have them put their hats on. Gather kids back together in a large group, and say: **Now let's begin our celebration by singing a song to thank God for making each of us special.** Have kids sing "Psalm 139:14" *(Group's Singable Songs for Children's Ministry).* After the song, lead kids in a short prayer, thanking God for creating them with special talents and abilities. Collect party hats for use later on.

POINT

Tracing Traits

Say: **Let's take some time to think about some of the qualities that make each of us special.** Have kids form pairs of one older child and one younger child. Give each pair two sheets of butcher paper and markers. Say: **In your pairs, take turns lying down on a sheet of butcher paper while your partner traces all the way around you.** Most kids will need to curl up in a fetal position in order to fit on the paper.

Give kids a few minutes to trace their patterns. Then have kids decorate their patterns using the markers. Make sure kids write their names on their patterns. Then display the patterns around your meeting area either by taping them to a wall or laying them on the floor around the edges of your meeting space. Say: **In a few minutes, we'll decorate each other's patterns with drawings and words that say something good about each person. But first let's think about some of the things that make people special.** Have kids brainstorm about qualities and characteristics they think make people special, and write them down on a chalkboard, dry-erase board, or sheet of newsprint. Say: **Now use this list to help you think of something special about each person here. When you've thought about something for a person, think of a word or a drawing that would show that characteristic. For example, if you think someone is a helpful person, write the word "helpful" on their pattern or draw a picture of someone helping another person. Think of one picture or word for each other person here, and draw or write on each person's pattern. Partners can help each other.** Give kids a few minutes to do this. Circulate around the

TEACHER TIP

If you have a large group of children, have them first form age-level groups to complete this project. Then have them form pairs within the age-level groups. Encourage kids to complete the project with only those children in their age-level groups. Make sure you have at least one adult helper with each group.

group, helping kids think of good qualities and find pictures or words to demonstrate those qualities. After kids finish, point out how these posters help us see that God made everyone special.

Guess What I'm Like

TEACHER TIP

For a large group, adapt this game in the following ways: Have your group form an even number of teams, making sure everyone is on a team. Have adult helpers each take two teams to separate areas of your meeting space. Have groups play several games of Charades simultaneously, and then bring groups back together to form one large group. Or pretend this game is a game show. Select two teams of kids to be the contestants who play the game and the rest of your group to represent the studio audience. Invite the audience to clap and cheer as the game progresses.

Gather kids into a large group, and say: **We're going to play a fun party game—Charades.** Have kids form two teams. Give each team three slips of paper and a pen or pencil. Say: **Pick one person on your team to be the writer. The writer will write on the slips of paper special characteristics of people that the other team will need to act out and guess. The things you write need to be some of the good qualities we've talked about today or any others you can think of. For example, you might write, "kind," "helpful," and "smart" on your slips of paper. Then someone from your team will act out a characteristic the other team has chosen. Your team will try to guess what that characteristic is. For example, if the characteristic you have to act out is "helpful," you might pretend to do helpful things for the people on your team.** When teams have finished writing on their paper slips, have them give their slips to you. Be sure to keep each team's slips separate from the other team's. Choose one team to go first, and have that team choose the person who will act out a quality first. Have that person draw one of the slips of paper from the opposing team's slips. Give the child one minute to act out the quality while his or her team tries to guess what it is. After one minute, give the other team a turn. Continue the game until all of the slips have been used. Not everyone will have a turn acting. If you have time or if your group is small, have teams make enough slips so that each person has a turn.

When the game is finished, call kids together, and ask:

● **Was it hard to guess the quality your team member was acting out? Why? Why not?**

● **How do we know what special qualities God gave people when he made them?**

Say: **God made everything in the world, and God made each of us. God made us special. We find out about the special qualities God gave others by the things they do. We've done some fun things today to help us think about all of the special qualities we have. Let's continue our birthday celebration.**

PRAYER

Priceless Presents

Before the session, cut apart the squares on the "God Made Me

Special" handout (p. 36). Punch a hole in each square, string a piece of ribbon through the hole, and tie the ribbon to a lollipop. You'll need to make one for each child.

Have kids sit in a circle, and say: **One of the best things about a birthday party is the presents. Each of you will get a present today. But instead of keeping the present, you will give your present to someone else in our group.** Give each child a card and lollipop you prepared before the session. Point out the words written on the card. Say: **We've talked about many ways God made each of us special. I'd like you to think of one way God made the person on your right special. In a minute, we'll go around the circle, and each person will say a short prayer, thanking God for a special quality in the person to his or her right. For example, you might say, "God, thank you for making** (name a child) **special by giving her** (or him) **a great smile." After you say your prayer, give that person your lollipop. Take a minute to think of a special quality of the person on your right.** Start the prayer, and have kids go around the circle saying prayers. When it gets back to you, close with "amen."

TEACHER TIP

For a large group, send the kids back to the groups they formed for the game of Charades. Have them do the activity as written in the smaller groups. Ask an adult helper to lead each group in the activity.

Happy Birthday!

Say: **No birthday party is complete without birthday cake.** Set out undecorated cupcakes, bowls of frosting with plastic knives, sprinkles, and napkins. Give kids the party hats they made at the beginning of the session. Invite kids to decorate their own cupcakes. As they're finishing, say: **Before we eat our birthday cake, let's sing "Happy Birthday to You." When it comes to the part of the song where you sing someone's name, sing "everyone" instead.**

Let kids eat their cupcakes. Remind kids to take their party hats and lollipops home.

TIME STRETCHER

Follow the Leader

Have kids put on their party hats and play a game of Follow the Leader. Choose one child to start as the leader, and let kids "parade" around the room. Change leaders every thirty seconds. Play until everyone has had a chance to lead.

For a large group, have kids form four groups. Have each group play its own game of Follow the Leader in its own section of the meeting area.

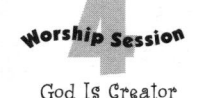

God Made Me Special

God made me special.	**God made me special.**
God made me special.	**God made me special.**
God made me special.	**God made me special.**
God made me special.	**God made me special.**

God Is Rest

HOW TO USE THIS WORSHIP SESSION

Use this session to help kids reflect on God as a God who understands the need for rest. Use this session close to Labor Day (observed in the U.S. and Canada).

OBJECTIVES

Kids will
- discover the signs of busyness and how it affects us,
- understand what God says about rest and relaxation, and
- celebrate God's design for rest.

YOU'LL NEED

- a Bible
- various cleaning supplies for cleaning projects
- poster board
- markers
- *Group's Singable Songs for Children's Ministry* (See index on pp. 121-122.)

BIBLE BASIS

Genesis 1–2:3 and Mark 6:30-32

The concept of work causes different emotions in people. For most kids, work is not something they look forward to. But God gave us work so we can accomplish the things needed to make our lives and world better. But he also gave us rest.

Genesis 1–2:3 is the biblical account of God's creation of the world. Through his work in creation, God shows us an example of how we should work and rest. The Bible tells us God worked for six days and rested on the seventh day. God shows us how to work and shows us what kind of work is best for us. And he teaches us how to rest. He told us the day of rest was just as important as the days of work. When we teach this Bible story to kids, we have the opportunity to show them how important both work and rest are in our lives.

Mark 6:30-32 tells a story of Jesus' concern for his disciples' need for rest. The Bible says they had been so busy that they hadn't time to eat. Jesus provides an example of a balanced life. He knew the importance of work, and he knew there were times when it was

THE
POINT
God wants us to
rest and relax.

important to rest. Help kids understand they need balanced lives, too. Show your kids Jesus' example, and share with them examples from your personal experience.

As you plan this worship session, take time to listen to God and what he tells each of us about the need for rest. Praise him for making rest an important part of his desire for our lives.

UNDERSTANDING YOUR KIDS

Kids are busy these days. They run from school to soccer practice to music lessons and then home to schoolwork. We need to help kids see that the key to self-worth is not through busyness, but through a balanced life with God, including meaningful work and rest.

God created work for us so we can take care of our world and develop our gifts and talents. God wants kids to work and to rest. Use this worship session to help kids discover the pitfalls of busyness and understand that part of God's plan for us is times of rest and relaxation, from a good night's sleep to a quiet Saturday morning.

PRAISE

Cleanup Time

Before the session, devise several simple cleaning jobs your group can do in your meeting area or in close proximity to your meeting area. This might be wiping down the tables with water and a cleanser or wiping off the chairs. You might want to check with your church's custodian to see what jobs might be available. Set out the required cleaning supplies before kids arrive.

After kids arrive, gather them in the large group, and say: **Today we're going to do some work. Our meeting area could use some sprucing up, so we're going to do some cleaning work.** Assign jobs to different groups of kids according to their abilities. Give them a reasonable amount of time to finish their jobs. When the jobs are done, have kids put the cleaning supplies in a designated spot, and have the group sit together on the floor. Say: **Wow! You worked really hard. You must feel like you need a rest now.** Ask:

● **Did you like the work I had you do? Why?**

● **How do you feel when someone tells you to do some work?**

Say: **Even though sometimes we'd rather play than work, work is important. Nothing will ever get done if no one ever works. We wouldn't have any food or clothes or medicine. Now lie back on the floor and close your eyes. Relax and rest after all the hard work you did.** Let children rest for a few seconds; then ask the group to sit up. Ask:

- **Why is it important for us to rest sometimes?**
- **What are some ways we rest and relax?**

A Resting Day

Say: **God needs to rest too. After he worked to create the world, he made a special day to rest and relax. Let's sing a song about a special day God made and praise him for wanting us to rest and relax sometimes.** Sing "This Is the Day" *(Group's Singable Songs for Children's Ministry)*. If you want to sing the song as a round, have kids form two groups, and have one group echo the other.

Say: **We have many reasons to be joyful and praise God. But today we praise God because he gives us time to rest and be quiet. God gives us those times because he also takes time to rest and be quiet. When God created the world, he worked for six days and made everything. But on the seventh day, he rested.** Read aloud Genesis 2:2. Say: **Find a partner, and tell him or her how you think God rested on that seventh day after he had worked so hard to make the world and the universe. Then tell your partner how you like to rest after you have worked really hard.** Give kids a chance to share, and then draw their attention back to you. Ask kids to share some of their ideas with the group.

Say: **Let's praise God for giving us time to rest from all the busyness in our lives and the hard work we do.** Lead kids in a prayer, thanking God for giving us the ability to enjoy work and enjoy rest and relaxation.

POINT

Always in a Hurry

As you teach this section of the session, do everything in a hurry and hurry kids along through their projects.

Have kids form pairs or trios depending on the size of your group. Give each group a piece of poster board and markers. Speaking faster than normal, say: **God tells us rest and relaxation are important in our lives. I want to introduce you to some people who might need to know this. Their names are "Busy Brianna" and "Gotta-Go Gary." Draw a picture of either one of these characters in the center of your sheet of poster board.** Give kids less time than usual to complete this. Say: **Now draw a clock face around these characters, putting a twelve at the top and a six at the bottom. Fill in the rest of the numbers as you see them on a clock.** Rush kids through this. Say: **In your groups, think of different activities that might keep Brianna, Gary, or other kids your**

TEACHER TIP

If your meeting space doesn't have enough room for kids to lie back on the floor, just have them sit and close their eyes.

TEACHER TIP

If you have a large group of kids, randomly select some posters to share with the rest of the group. You may not have time to show them all. Also have kids get back into their small groups to make facilitating the discussion easier. Ask the questions, and have the kids discuss the questions in their groups. If you have enough adult helpers, ask them to sit with the small groups and lead the discussion.

age busy, and draw them at the time of day they do these activities. For example, you might draw a soccer ball at three o'clock or homework at seven o'clock. Make sure you fill up your poster with activities because these are very busy people. While kids are working on their posters, keep telling them to hurry up because you have many other activities for them to do. When time is up, gather kids together and have them show their posters.

Ask:

● **What will happen if Brianna and Gary are this busy every day?**

● **What do you think they will say if someone tells them they should take time to rest?**

● **How did you feel while you were doing this project?**

● **How do you feel when you have too many things to do or when other people in your family are rushing around all the time?**

● **Are there times when you've felt like Brianna and Gary? When?**

● **What do you think God thinks when we don't take time to rest?**

Jesus' Friends Rest

Open your Bible to Mark 6:30-32. Say: **Even Jesus, God's Son, knew it was important to rest. Let's hear a story about Jesus. Every time I say, "The disciples were very busy," I want you to say, "I think they need to rest." Let's practice saying that.** Have the kids practice saying that phrase; then tell the following story. Say: **Jesus gave his disciples special jobs to do. The disciples were very busy.** Pause for kids to respond. **He sent them to different towns and villages to tell people about God. The disciples were very busy.** Pause for kids to respond. **They preached to lots of people, and they healed many people who were sick. The disciples were very busy.** Pause for kids to respond. **Soon it was time for them to go back to where Jesus was. They packed up their things, said goodbye to the people they had met, and started out on their journey. The disciples were very busy.** Pause for kids to respond. **When they saw Jesus, they were excited to tell him everything that had happened to them. They all wanted to talk at once and have Jesus' attention. The disciples were very busy.** Pause for kids to respond. **But there were a lot of other people around who wanted to talk to Jesus, too. They wanted to ask him questions and have him heal their illnesses. Jesus gave the disciples jobs to do to help care for these people. The disciples were very busy.** Pause for kids to respond. **The disciples had so much to do that they didn't even have a chance to eat lunch. Jesus noticed that his friends were beginning to look tired and**

worn out. **Jesus gathered his friends around him and said, "You've been working very hard. You need some rest. Come away with me to a quiet place so we can relax." Jesus knew rest was important.** After you finish telling the story, ask:

● **What kinds of things kept the disciples so busy?**

● **Do you think the tasks the disciples were involved in were important? Why or why not?**

● **Why do you think Jesus wanted them to rest?**

● **What does this story tell us about our need for rest and relaxation?**

Say: **The disciples did good things. In order for them to keep doing good things, though, Jesus knew they needed to get some rest. It's the same for us. Most of the things that keep us really busy are good things, but in order for us to be healthy and to keep our lives balanced, we need rest and relaxation. This is what God wants for us.**

PRAYER

Resting With God

Have kids sit on the floor. Say: **When we rest and are quiet, we can think about God more clearly than when we are busy and distracted. That's one of the reasons God likes us to rest. We're going to sing a quiet song that talks about focusing on God.** Lead kids in singing the first verse of "Seek Ye First" *(Group's Singable Songs for Children's Ministry)*. Sing the song a few times, and then ask:

● **How do you feel when you sing a quiet song?**

● **What do you think "Seek ye first the kingdom of God" means?**

● **How does resting help us seek God's kingdom?**

● **What does the song say will happen if we seek God's kingdom? What do you think that means?**

Say: **The words of this song come from a Bible verse. These are words Jesus said. God wants us to work, but God wants us to spend time with him, too. Sometimes the best times we have with God are when we are quiet and resting.** Have kids get into a comfortable position in which they feel relaxed. Ask them to close their eyes and block out any distractions. Say: **I'm going to ask you some questions about God. Don't answer them out loud, but think about your answers to the questions.** Ask:

● **Think about Bible stories you know. What is your favorite story about something God did? Why is that your favorite story?**

After each question or statement, give kids a short time to think in silence about their answers or responses.

● **Think about a time God answered one of your prayers. Thank God for doing that for you.**

● **Thank God for creating something you really enjoy.**

● **What is something you need in your life right now? Take a few seconds and talk to God about that need.**

● **Thank God for helping us understand how important rest is. Ask God to help us take time to think about him.**

Close this quiet time with a short prayer, thanking God for his example of rest and asking God's help in balancing rest and our busy lives.

Gather kids back together, and ask:

● **How did it feel to spend those few minutes of rest and silence with God?**

● **How can you find time during the next week to do this again?**

Sabbath Special

Say: **God knew it would be hard for us to find time to spend with him because of our busy lives. That's why God made a special day of rest called the Sabbath. It's a special day when we take time to focus on God. We learn about who God is and what God wants us to do. We sang a song at the beginning of this worship session about rejoicing in a special day. Let's sing that song again to thank God for creating the Sabbath.** Sing the song; then close with a prayer, thanking God for giving us a special day to think about God and to worship him.

TIME STRETCHER

Chill Coupons

Have kids make "chill" coupon books for their families and themselves that will help them slow down their hectic lifestyles.

Write Genesis 2:3 and Mark 6:31 on a chalkboard, dry-erase board, or sheet of newsprint that's taped to a wall. Give each child two pieces of colored construction paper, markers, and scissors. Have kids cut each piece of construction paper into fourths. On four of the sections, have kids write one of the Bible verses; on the other four sections, have kids write the other Bible verse.

Then have kids write on the back of each piece a different activity they like to do as a family—for example, playing a game, going to the park, or eating out at a fast-food restaurant. When kids have finished, they'll have listed eight different activities.

Say: **Take these coupons home, and put them in a jar. Explain to your family what they are. Whenever someone in your family**

feels stressed or overly busy, pull out a coupon, and have everyone agree to have a little time to relax as you do this activity together as a family.

God Provides for All Our Needs

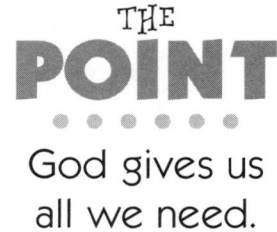

THE POINT

God gives us all we need.

HOW TO USE THIS WORSHIP SESSION

Use this session at Thanksgiving or any time you want kids to focus on being thankful.

OBJECTIVES

Kids will
- discover many things they're thankful for,
- learn that God provides us with everything we need, and
- express thankfulness to God.

YOU'LL NEED

- a Bible
- scratch paper
- pencils
- several large tree branches or an artificial Christmas tree
- construction paper
- markers
- scissors
- a hole punch
- string or yarn
- dried corn kernels or popcorn kernels
- a 6x6-inch square of burlap or other fabric for each child
- ribbon
- *Group's Singable Songs for Children's Ministry* (See index on pp. 121-122.)

BIBLE BASIS

Luke 17:11-19 and Philippians 4:4-6, 19

The Thanksgiving season is a time of year when we take time to reflect on all of the blessings we have in our lives and offer God a hearty "Thank you!"

The story found in Luke 17:11-19 of the ten men who had leprosy demonstrates that our loving God does, indeed, provide everything we need, including our very lives and health. The story serves as a

reminder that we, just as the one leper who returned, should recognize the need to be deeply and profoundly thankful.

Philippians 4:4-6, 19 reminds us that we can always trust God to meet our needs. We may not always understand God's plan or be able to see the big picture, but we can always trust God completely, knowing that his plan for our lives is perfect. Thus we can truly "rejoice in the Lord always."

UNDERSTANDING YOUR KIDS

As any parent who has ever tried to get a child to write after-Christmas thank you notes knows, expressing gratitude and thankfulness doesn't always come naturally to a child. We can help kids learn to demonstrate honest and sincere thankfulness by pointing out all of the amazing gifts God gives them each day.

We can take the concept of thanksgiving one step further by remembering Paul's timeless words found in Philippians. Although Paul was in prison and his future looked bleak, he still demonstrated an unwavering trust in God's plan. He even went so far as to thank God for his present circumstances, knowing that God would bring good from bad. Through this, we can help kids see that trust in God and thankfulness to God go hand in hand.

PRAISE

Sensing Thanks

Sing "Everybody Give Thanks!" *(Group's Singable Songs for Children's Ministry).* Sing the song once, and then have kids form five multi-age groups. Give each group a piece of scratch paper and a pencil. Assign each group one of the five senses: smell, taste, touch, sight, and hearing. Say: **In your groups, I'd like you to think of as many things as you can that you're thankful for that go along with the sense I assigned you. For example, if you are in the "smell" group, you might list the smell of cookies baking or the smell of bubble bath. Each group needs to choose one person who will write down everything your group thinks of. Take a few minutes to talk about this. Ready? Go!** Give kids a few minutes, and then say: **Time's up. Now we're going to thank God for all of the good things our groups thought of. We're going to do this in a praise litany. After groups each share something they're thankful for, say, "Thank you, God, for all your gifts." Let's practice that. Ready? Thank you, God, for all your gifts. Now let's start with the "smell" group. Tell us all of the things God gives us that we can smell.** When kids in this group are finished, lead everyone in the response. Continue in this manner until all groups have shared. Then say: **Wow! We have so many things to be thankful for because**

TEACHER TIP

If you have a large group, you may need to have kids form more than five groups. Simply double up on the senses, allowing more than one group to explore each sense.

God gives us everything we need. Let's show our thanks by singing "Everybody Give Thanks!" one more time.

Rejoice Always

Have kids sing "Rejoice in the Lord Always" *(Group's Singable Songs for Children's Ministry).* Have kids sing the song once and then form groups to sing the song again in a round. Ask:

● **What do you think it means to "rejoice in the Lord always"?**

Say: **I'd like to share with you the passage in the Bible where this song comes from. This passage is actually part of a letter the Apostle Paul wrote to his friends, the Philippians, when he was in jail.** Open your Bible to Philippians 4:4, and show the passage to the kids. Say: **The first line is just like our song. It says, "Rejoice in the Lord always."** Ask:

● **What are some things we do when we rejoice?**

Say: **Further on in the Bible, Paul wrote to his friends, "Do not be anxious about anything."** Ask:

● **Can you show me what you look like when you're anxious or worried?**

Say: **Next the Bible says, "In everything, by prayer and petition, with thanksgiving, present your requests to God." This tells us that God wants us to do two things when we pray: First he wants us to thank him for all of the good things he gives us. Second he wants us to ask him for the things we need. Now show me some things people do when they pray.** Kids may kneel, bow their heads, or fold their hands. Say: **Another part of Paul's letter says, "And my God will meet all your needs according to his glorious riches in Christ Jesus." What an amazing promise God gives us! He always gives us everything we need. We have many, many reasons to give thanks to him. Let's sing our song one more time.** Sing "Rejoice in the Lord Always" again.

POINT

One Man Gives Thanks

Say: **Today we're talking about giving thanks to God for all the things he gives us. We have a holiday we celebrate in the fall during which we spend time with our families and friends, giving thanks and remembering everything God has done for us during the past year.** Ask:

● **What holiday am I talking about?**

Say: **That's right—it's Thanksgiving!** Ask:

● **What are some of the things your family does to celebrate Thanksgiving?**

Say: **Early Thanksgiving feasts were to celebrate God's gifts** and provisions. **Now we're going to learn about a thankful person in the Bible. This story comes from the book of Luke. I'll need your help to tell this story.** Choose one person to be Jesus, nine people to be lepers, one person to be the thankful leper, and several kids to be priests. If you have more kids than there are parts, have them be audience members who clap and cheer or boo according to the actions.

Say: **Now listen for your part while I tell the story, and do what I say.**

One day Jesus was walking to Jerusalem. Suddenly he heard a group of ten people who had leprosy, a skin disease. They were calling out to him. They cried, "Jesus, Master, have pity on us!" They wanted Jesus to take away their dreadful disease and make them well.

When Jesus saw them and heard their cries, he said, "Go, show yourselves to the priests." So the ten lepers went to see the priests. While the lepers were with the priests, they were suddenly completely healed.

After they were healed, nine of the ten lepers went back to their homes, shouting and rejoicing. The tenth leper came back to Jesus and threw himself at Jesus' feet. He thanked Jesus with all of his heart for making him well. Jesus told the man, "Rise and go; your faith has made you well."

After the story, have kids give themselves a round of applause. Ask:

● **Which one of the lepers did the right thing? Why?**

● **Why do you think only one of the lepers came back to say thank you to Jesus?**

● **Why do you think it was important for the one leper to tell Jesus how thankful he was?**

Say: **God gives each of us everything we need. We need to always remember to say thank you just as one leper went back to thank Jesus.**

PRAYER

Thanking Tree

Before the session, use the large tree branches to form a tree that's leaning against a wall or is free-standing; or set up the artificial Christmas tree.

Say: **We're going to create a thanking tree that will remind us that God gives us everything we need.** Ask:

● **How do trees remind you of God?**

Say: **One of the ways trees are like God is that they are very strong. A tree can stand up to all kinds of weather—wind, hot**

TEACHER TIP

To make the craft part of this activity more manageable for a large group, station several adult helpers among the kids to distribute supplies and help with the project.

TEACHER TIP

If you want to avoid a writing activity entirely, have magazine pictures and glue available. Kids can choose pictures of things they're thankful for and glue them to the leaves.

sunshine, rain, and even snow—and they still provide us with shade, leaves, and sometimes even fruit. God is the same way. Even in tough times, he always provides us with everything we need.

Now let's make "leaves" for this tree in the shape of our hands, and we'll use the leaves to show God our thankfulness.

Distribute construction paper, markers, scissors, and pencils. Have each child trace one of his or her hands on a piece of construction paper and then cut out the tracing. You may want to have older kids help the younger ones. Say: **On your leaf, write or draw a short letter to God that talks about several things you're thankful for. You might list things like your family, food to eat, or a house to live in.** Give kids a few minutes to write or draw their letters. Then help kids punch holes in their leaves, tie string or yarn through the holes, and hang the leaves on the tree.

After kids have hung the leaves on the tree, say: **Each time we look at this tree or any tree, we can remember that God, in his strength, gives us everything we need.**

Giving Thanks

Say: **Now we'll make a reminder of all God gives us that you can take home with you. A long time ago when people ate Thanksgiving dinner together, they would put five grains of corn at each person's plate. The five grains of corn reminded people of the first Thanksgiving dinner** [Children's Ministry Magazine, November/December 1997]. **The early settlers were very thankful for food, their families, and their lives. We'll make a bundle of five grains of corn. You can take these home as a reminder to be thankful—to tell God "thank you" for giving us everything we need. You may want to tell your parents about the five grains of corn, and you can use this tradition in your home at Thanksgiving or at any family meal.** Give each child five dried corn kernels, a square of burlap, and a piece of ribbon. Have kids place the corn kernels on the burlap, make a bundle, and then tie the burlap shut with the ribbon.

End your time together with a prayer similar to this one: **Dear God, thank you so much for giving us everything we need. Please give us open hearts so we will remember to always say thank you. In Jesus' name, amen.**

TIME STRETCHER

Biscuit-Dough Pretzels

For this activity, you'll need refrigerated biscuit dough and cookie sheets.

Give each child a pre-formed biscuit; then have kids form dough into pretzels. Tell kids that pretzels can symbolize praying hands, and have kids offer short prayers of thanksgiving. Bake the pretzels, and have children each express their thankfulness that God has provided everything they need by sharing a pretzel with someone else.

God Is Truthful

THE POINT

God never lies.

HOW TO USE THIS WORSHIP SESSION

Use this session to teach kids that they can always believe what God says.

OBJECTIVES

Kids will
- praise God for being truthful,
- discover why it's important to tell the truth, and
- learn that God's Word is always truthful.

YOU'LL NEED

- Bibles
- a taped-up sheet of newsprint or an overhead transparency
- markers
- two bowls of salt
- plastic spoons
- 11x17 pieces of construction paper in light colors
- masking tape
- a long sheet of newsprint (Heavy white butcher paper works better if it's available.)

BIBLE BASIS

Isaiah 45:19; John 8:31-32; 14:6-7; and 15:26

Jesus lived in a confused world where God's truth had gotten lost. The scribes and Pharisees spoke of having the truth. People listened to them and followed their directions. Rules and regulations, after all, must be the truth God wanted them to know. Follow those rules, and you could be a holy person and live close to God.

Good news was needed—good news that turned people's lives upside down, shook out the false ideas, and made them ready for real truth. Throughout Jesus' ministry—particularly in the teaching found in the book of John—Jesus tells his followers again and again, "I tell you the truth..." It is life-changing, spirit-filling, mind-cleansing, heart-opening truth. When people hear it from Jesus, they feel a radical upheaval. God takes hold of them through Jesus, bringing them into the new kingdom.

Even before the coming of Jesus, the prophet Isaiah delivered the

message of God's truth. It was a stinging reality, and many shut their ears to it. But Isaiah faithfully shared a message that the God of Israel is the source of truth and will always declare what is right and good for God's people. A few listened, but most shut their ears. The crush of Babylon was swift. The prophet's words echoed loudly as God's people were taken into captivity.

UNDERSTANDING YOUR KIDS

We live in a time when many things masquerade as the truth. Images that look like the truth bombard children. Their ears fill with words that seem to be the truth. How do they decide what's true, anyway?

Kids faithfully follow their parents. Kids want to please their parents and to believe them. Kids also follow their friends and want to please them. They take at face value what others say to them— especially adults. They believe a TV commercial that tells them a certain toy is the best there is. The world of a child is very concrete. They're learning how to determine what's truthful and what isn't.

When we anchor children in God's truth, we give them a wonderful gift. In that truth they find comfort, support, answers, and stability. Even when everything in their world falls apart, they know that what God says is always true. They'll face many lies, but they'll know that God never lies. What an incredible honor to bring that good news to a child.

Use this worship session as a way of introducing the richness and the glory of God's truth to your kids. Your absolute belief in that truth will be a huge part of the learning process. After all, your kids trust you. Take their hands and journey together as you explore God's wonderful truth.

PRAISE

It's True

Before the session, write on the taped-up sheet of newsprint or on the overhead transparency the following words to a song:

> **Truth, truth, God is truth.**
> **We can trust God's Word.**
> **Every time we read God's book,**
> **We can learn the truth.**

Welcome the kids, and gather them together. Tell them to look at the words on the newsprint or transparency. Say: **Today we're going to learn that God always tells the truth. Every time we read something God tells us in the Bible, we know it's true. We never have to doubt God. How many of you know how to sing "Row,**

"Row, Row Your Boat"? Let's sing that song together.** Sing the song until everyone—even the younger children—knows the tune.

Read aloud the new words written on the newsprint. Ask the kids to sing those words to the tune of "Row, Row, Row Your Boat." Sing the song through until all the children know the new words.

Say: **That was great! Now here's what we're going to do. I want you each to think about a time last week when you told the truth about something. For example, maybe a teacher asked a question and you knew the answer. That was telling the truth. Maybe a parent asked you if you'd cleaned your room and you told the truth about that. When you think of something you told the truth about, raise your hand. We'll sing the song again, and then I will point to some of you who have your hands raised. When I point to you, stand up and tell us about the time you told the truth. I'll point to two or three people, and then we'll sing the song again.** Sing the song, and have children share several times so all who want a turn can have one. Ask:

● **How do you feel when you tell the truth?**

● **How do you feel when you tell a lie?**

● **What happens to you when you get caught telling a lie? Why?**

Say: **The song we just sang says we can always trust God's Word because God always tells the truth. That means everything Jesus told us about God is true. Jesus is God's Son, and Jesus always tells the truth. Jesus hopes we will always tell the truth, too, but he knows it's really hard sometimes. When we do mess up and tell a lie, we don't feel good about it. That helps us want to tell the truth the next time. Guess what? Even if we tell a lie, God will forgive us if we ask God to do that.**

TEACHER TIP

For larger groups, have children form multiple circles; then ask an adult helper to sit with each circle and lead this activity.

The True Book

Sit together with the kids in a circle. Place a Bible in the center of the circle. Ask one child to get the Bible and give it to another child in the circle. When the first child hands the Bible to someone, ask him or her to say, "Here's a present of God's truth for you." Ask the child who receives the Bible to then get up and give it to someone else in the circle, saying the same words. Continue around the circle until each child has received and given the Bible to someone else. The last person to get the Bible should give it to you. Ask:

● **How did you feel when someone gave you the Bible?**

● **How did you feel when you gave the Bible to someone else?**

Say: **We discover God's truth in two ways. Sometimes we find the answers ourselves when we read the Bible. Sometimes we help others find God's truth by sharing with them what the Bible says. Let's pray together: Dear God, thank you for the Bible.**

When we read it, we know that what it says is truthful. Thank you for sending Jesus to tell us the truth. It's in his name that we pray. Amen.

POINT

Is It Really True?

On a table, set out the two bowls of salt and several spoons. Gather the kids in a group near the table. Say: **Every day you hear or see things that make you wonder if it's the truth or not. What's something you have seen or heard and then wondered if it was true? For example, I saw a TV ad that told me if I bought a special cream and put it on my face every night, I would never have any wrinkles. I wonder if that was true. Who wants to go next?** Wait for a kids to respond.

Say: **Sometimes it's hard to know whether something we hear or see is the truth or not. Sometimes the truth and a lie look the same, but we have to decide. Let's have an experience together to see what I mean. On the table are two bowls. One might have sugar in it, and the other might have salt in it. But they both look the same. I'm not going to tell you what's in the bowls. Here's the deal: If you think you know what's in the bowls, I'll let you go to the table and take some in one of the spoons. Don't eat it yet— just carry it back in the spoon and sit down. When all our volunteers make their choice, I'll let you eat what you have in your spoon. Then we'll see who ended up with what.**

Let kids volunteer to go get a small amount from one of the bowls. Don't let kids shake the bowls or smell them. They have to make their choice by looking at the bowls. Remind kids that whatever they put in their spoon, they have to eat later.

When everyone who sampled from the two bowls sits back down, have them taste what's in their spoons. Don't react to what happens. Simply ask what they had in their spoons. Soon kids will figure out that no one got any sugar because both bowls have salt in them. Ask:

● **How do you feel right now?**

● **How could you tell if it was sugar or salt in the bowl?**

● **Describe another time you couldn't tell if something was really what it seemed to be?**

Say: **I told you one of the bowls might have sugar in it and one of the bowls might have salt in it. I got away with that because sugar and salt both look the same. All you had to do was try to make the right choice. You see, things are not always what they appear to be. Sometimes we need to test things to see if they're really true. If I had let you touch or move the bowls, you**

TEACHER TIP

If you have a large group, you can use this activity as an object lesson. Have kids remain in the large group, seated in chairs or on the floor. Use the "say" statements given, instructing children to test what is in the bowls. Then invite a few volunteers from the large group to test the bowls' contents.

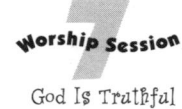

might have been able to figure out that both bowls have salt in them. Not everything we are told stands up to the truth test. It's hard to know what's true sometimes. But God's truth always passes the test. God never tells us something that isn't true—never! Whatever God tells us in the Bible is always the truth. We never have to doubt it.

Read aloud John 8:31-32. Ask:

● **What did Jesus say we had to do in order to know the truth?**

● **What did Jesus say would happen to us when we know the truth about something?**

● **What do you think that means?**

● **Why do you think people sometimes lie to us?**

● **How would you feel if you thought God sometimes lied to you?**

Say: **As long as we listen to what God and Jesus say in the Bible, we will always know the truth. We never have to worry about being lied to by God, and this helps us feel free to believe the Bible.**

Truth Protection

Have kids form multi-age groups of four or five. Give each group five sheets of lightly colored construction paper, a marker, and a Bible. Ask the oldest member of each group to read the following Bible passages to the group: John 14:6-7 and 15:26. When kids finish reading, ask the groups to discuss the following questions:

● **What three ways did Jesus describe himself in John 14:6-7?**

● **Who did Jesus call the Holy Spirit in John 15:26?**

Gain the attention of all the groups, and say: **Jesus tells us he is the truth from God. He also tells us the Holy Spirit is the truth from God. There's no changing that. Jesus and the Holy Spirit are both God's truth for us. That's good news. Each group has five sheets of paper. Decide in your small group five things you believe are true about God. In other words, what do you know to be the absolute truth about God? For example, someone in your group might say, "I believe that God always loves me, no matter what." That's something you could write on one of your sheets. Another person might say, "I believe that God always hears my prayers." You could write that on one of your sheets of construction paper. Decide together five things you believe about God or Jesus that are always true. Have someone in your group write one item on each sheet of construction paper.**

When the groups finish their work, gather everyone in a large circle. Have kids sit in the circle with the other members of their group. Ask each group to lay its five sheets of construction paper on the floor in front of the group. Ask each group to share its list.

TEACHER TIP

With a large group, do this activity by having the group form smaller age-level groups. For example, put your kindergartners and first-graders together in one group, second- and third-graders together, and so on. Have kids form age-level groups of four to five. Younger kids can draw pictures of God's truth, or an adult volunteer can help them write their ideas. Ask adult helpers to supervise each age-level group.

After all the groups have shared, arrange the sheets of paper side by side so they form a large square. Ask some of the kids to help you tape all of them together with masking tape. Have some of the kids hold up the taped sheets while the rest of the group gathers underneath them. Then have the kids holding the corners slide in underneath. Everyone should now be under the sheets of paper. Ask:

- **How do you feel, being covered by all of these things that are true about God?**

- **In what ways do you feel protected by these things we know are true about God?**

Say: **We can always count on God to be there for us. These sheets protect us because they have God's truth written on them. God's truth protects us because it shows us the right way to live. No one can take that truth away from us. The more we read and study the Bible, the more we learn about God and Jesus. That helps us know the truth. It's a good feeling to have God's truth on our side and to be protected by it.**

PRAYER

Breaking Through

Roll out a long sheet of newsprint or butcher paper on the floor. Ask the kids to gather around the paper in the small groups they formed in the last activity. Give each person a marker. Say: **We've learned a lot today about God's truth. A long time ago, one of God's prophets named Isaiah also told the people of Israel about God's truth.** Read aloud Isaiah 45:19, and then say: **It was a hard time in their history, and many of the people had forgotten to follow God's truth. Because of that, they were captured by the Babylonians, their enemies, and made to leave their homes. They wondered if God was still with them. Yes, God's truth was still there even though they had disobeyed God. Sometimes we lie and disobey God, but God still loves us. On the sheet of paper, write or draw symbols of things people sometimes lie about. For example, draw a picture of a cookie to illustrate a time you lied about taking a cookie off the kitchen table and eating it. Draw a picture of a toy you once saved money for because the television commercial told you it would last forever, but it broke the first week you had it. Or write, "My friend said she wanted to play with me, and then she never came over." Write or draw everything you can think of people lie about.** Each group should work on a portion of the length of paper.

When the groups finish working, ask a few kids to help you hold up the paper in front of the group. Ask children to each share one thing they put on the list. Say: **Wow, there's a lot of stuff people**

TEACHER TIP

For a large group, do this activity in the smaller age-level groups from the last activity.

TEACHER TIP

Make sure the markers will not bleed through the paper onto the floor below. If you think that could happen, put another layer of paper underneath the first layer.

lie about. We know that. We also know that when people lie to us, we can go to God for help. When we lie, we know that God will forgive us and help us to stop lying.

Ask two adult volunteers or two taller kids to hold the sheet or hang it between two posts. Line up the group five feet in front of the sheet. Make sure the little children are at one end and the older children are at the other end. Say: **We've learned that God never lies to us. We know that God's truth is always stronger than the lies on this paper. God wants us to break away from lying. When I say "go," I want everyone to walk quickly through the paper to break it apart. Let's break through those lies. Ready? Go!**

Then have the group sit on pieces of the torn paper. Pray the following prayer with the kids by saying each line and asking the kids to repeat the line after you. Say: **Dear God, thank you for always telling us the truth. We know we can always trust you. We know we can always trust Jesus. Help us to do the right thing when we want to tell a lie. You are always there for us. In Jesus' name, amen.**

TIME STRETCHER

My Faith Shield

Draw a large replica of the faith shield on a sheet of newsprint. Or draw a copy of the shield and make a photocopy of your drawing for each child. Have children form pairs to answer the questions. Ask older children to work with younger children. When the pairs finish, have kids discuss their answers as a large group. Tell them to take home their faith shields to remember that God's truth is always with them.

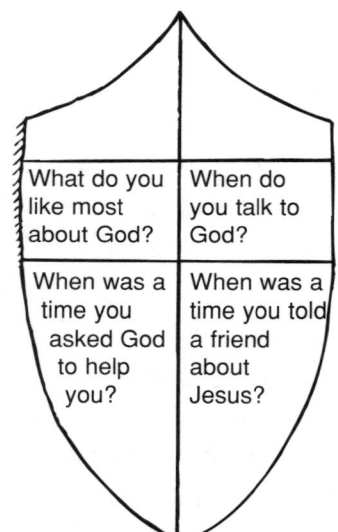

| What do you like most about God? | When do you talk to God? |
| When was a time you asked God to help you? | When was a time you told a friend about Jesus? |

God Is Joyful

HOW TO USE THIS WORSHIP SESSION

Use this session to help kids reflect on God's joyfulness.

OBJECTIVES

Kids will
- learn that God is joyful,
- determine which things please God,
- look for God in the things that bring them joy, and
- praise God for giving them joy and for being joyful.

YOU'LL NEED

- Bibles
- dry-erase markers
- streamers
- balloons
- markers
- masking tape
- a cassette or CD player
- a children's worship tape or CD
- *Group's Singable Songs for Children's Ministry* (See index on pp. 121-122.)

BIBLE BASIS

Psalm 8; James 1:17; and 1 John 4:9-10

"Be quiet! We're in church." "Will you please stop fidgeting and be respectful?" We've made a mistake. We've taught our kids that God is boring, quiet, and irritable. There is, of course, a time for reverence, a time to be silent, and a time to be still. But there is also a time for joy, celebration, and fun. Whether we like it or not, children associate their experiences in church with the character of God.

Children need to know that God is warm, joyful, and personally interested in them. There is no doubt God is beyond our understanding and imagination, but he is also intimate and tender with us. Psalm 8 gives a beautiful description of this paradox. God is majestic and has "set [his] glory above the heavens." Yet he is also "mindful" of us and has "crowned [us] with glory and honor."

James 1:17 says that every good and perfect gift comes from God. Joy, laughter, and fun are wonderful gifts from God. One only needs

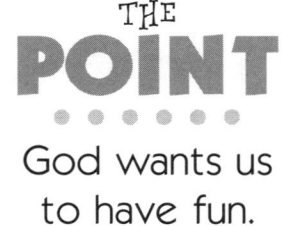

THE
POINT
· · · · · ·
God wants us
to have fun.

to look at God's gift of creation to find examples of his vibrancy, sense of humor, and joy.

God knows we need to laugh, to have fun, and experience joy. God provides joy for us because—as 1 John 4:9-10 clearly shows—he loves us dearly. Teach your kids that God is powerful, awesome, and someone to be revered. But also teach your kids that God is intimate, joyful, and fun.

UNDERSTANDING YOUR KIDS

Children live in a black-and-white world. They may have difficulties understanding that God is omnipotent *and* tender, omniscient *and* personally interested, omnipresent *and* intimately involved. As teachers, our challenge is to teach concrete truths about a seemingly enigmatic God.

Some of your children may be confused by this worship session. They are in touch with God's power and position but are unaware of his laughter and joy. Others may respond to this worship session with a casual "Of course God is joyful."

Use this session to help kids understand one of God's many attributes. As kids mature in their faith, they'll come to understand that God's character is multifaceted and beyond their complete comprehension.

PRAISE

Laugh Aloud

Say: **To start our meeting time, let's play a game of Laugh Aloud. The object of Laugh Aloud is to avoid laughing or even smiling.**

Have kids lie down on the floor so that they're using each other's stomachs as pillows (see the diagram in the margin). Make sure each child (except the last one) has only one head on his or her stomach.

Say: **To play Laugh Aloud, the person who is acting as the very bottom pillow must say, "Ha." Then the next person will say, "Ha, ha." The third person will say, "Ha, ha, ha," and so on until the last person has a chance to say his or her ha's. You can shake your belly when you say, "Ha," but you can't smile or laugh. If anyone smiles or laughs, the game will begin again. Are there any questions about playing Laugh Aloud?**

After you've answered questions, have kids begin playing the game. Keep playing until kids are able to go through the whole line without laughing, or play a few rounds starting at both ends of the line.

Have kids get into groups of four to discuss these questions:

● **Was it difficult or easy to keep yourself from laughing? Why?**

TEACHER TIP

With a large group, have children form several teams. Have each team form a line and lie down with heads on stomachs. Have teams play the game simultaneously.

- **What things make you laugh?**
- **Do you like to laugh? Why or why not?**
- **Do you think God laughs? Why or why not?**
- **How do you feel when you think about God?**

Say: **We all like to have fun, and we all like to laugh. But did you know that *God* wants us to have fun and that he likes to see us laugh? God doesn't want our relationship with him or our worship to be boring or meaningless. He wants it to be joyful and real. Let's worship God right now. While we sing, express your joy and laughter to God. You can clap your hands, stomp your feet, dance around, or just sing the words.**

Joyful Singing

Lead kids in two worship songs they think are especially fun and joyful. For example, sing "Down in My Heart" and "Ha-La-La-La" (*Group's Singable Songs for Children's Ministry*). Ask:

- **How did you like singing those songs?**
- **How do you like worshiping God? Explain.**
- **Is there any way worship could be a more joyful experience for you? If so, how?**
- **Do you believe God wants us to have fun? Why or why not?**

Lead kids in a prayer, thanking God for his joy and asking his help in our worship of him.

POINT

Delightful Drawings

Have kids get into pairs. Have children tell their partners the one thing they enjoy doing most with their families. Then have kids tell their partners the one thing they think God enjoys doing the most. As kids talk, give each pair a dry-erase marker.

Say: **I'd like you to draw pictures of the one thing in life that brings you the most joy. For example, you could draw a picture of your dog, your parents, going swimming, or worshiping God. These pictures will be very special because they'll show the joy you have *and* because we're going to draw them on windows around our building.**

Direct kids to the different windows they can use as canvases. Give very specific directions regarding the places kids can and cannot draw. Make sure you have enough adult supervision. After about five minutes, have kids gather together back in your meeting area.

Read aloud Psalm 8, and then have pairs discuss these questions:

- **What kinds of things bring joy to God?**
- **When do you think God is smiling at you?**

TEACHER TIP

If you don't have enough windows or enough markers for all the kids to use, give each child a crayon designed for use in the bathtub. These crayons will wash off most types of tile. Have kids draw their pictures on the floor or another tiled location in your church building.

Before the session, test the surfaces you plan to use (whether you're using dry-erase markers or erasable crayons) to make sure *all* of the pictures will erase. Make sure the conditions you test the marks under are the same as when kids will actually be doing the activity. For example, if the window you use will get a great deal of direct sunlight, make sure the marks will still erase after prolonged exposure to the sun.

If your church doesn't have windows or tile for kids to use, you could take the activity outside and give kids sidewalk chalk or use newsprint or poster board and markers within your meeting area.

PRAYER

TEACHER TIP

If your group is very large, you may have to direct children to different rooms. If kids have "home" rooms, have them go to those rooms with adult volunteers. Don't let kids wander off on their own.

TEACHER TIP

If you have a large group, decide on three or four games before the worship session. Set up game centers—one for each game—in various areas of your meeting space. Enlist several adult helpers to lead the games. Allow kids to choose the game they would like to play, making sure you have an even distribution of kids.

● **Do you see God as someone who is joyful or grumpy? Why?**

Say: **Do you know what makes God joyful? You do! But you don't have to take my word for it. Listen to what God says about you in the Bible.** Read aloud 1 John 4:9-10. Say: **Even when you make mistakes, God is happy he created you. God thinks you're wonderful and beautiful. God loves you and cares for you so much that he sent Jesus to die for you. God is joyful about you!** Ask:

● **What are some other things God is joyful about?**

Have kids return to the windows to create pictures of things they think bring joy to God. After about five minutes, have the kids return. Ask:

● **What pictures did you draw?**

● **Why did you draw them?**

Say: **Did you know both of the pictures you drew are things that make God joyful? God wants us to have fun—especially when the fun we have brings joy to us. God is joyful, and he loves it when we are joyful too! One way we can celebrate God's joy is by having fun. Let's do that right now.**

Giddy Games

Lead kids in a round of their favorite game. You might want to play Fruit Basket Upset; Duck, Duck, Goose; or Simon Says. If you're not sure what game to play, check out *Fun & Easy Games* (Group Publishing, Inc., 1998) for some ideas.

After the game, have kids form groups of four. Make sure each group has a person who is able to read. Give each group a Bible, and have groups discuss these questions:

● **Do you think God enjoyed watching us play this game? Why or why not?**

● **Read James 1:17. Why do you think God created laughter? fun? joy?**

● **What other gifts has God given us?**

PRAYER

Celebration of Joy

Have kids remain in their groups of four. Give each group streamers, balloons, markers, and tape. Say: **We're going to show God and other people who come into our meeting area the joy God has given us and the joy God has by decorating our space. On each decoration you hang up, you must use the markers to write or draw a prayer of thanksgiving or a word of praise. Write or draw messages to God telling him why you're thankful for who he is**

and the fun and joyful things he has given you to appreciate. For example, on a balloon write, "Thank you for laughter" to thank God. On a streamer draw a picture of birds singing to show that God has given us joyful songs to wake up to. Draw a picture of a heart to show that God loves us and wants us to have fun. After you write or draw your prayers on the decorations, tape the decorations around the meeting area.

While kids work, play upbeat worship music in the background.

After about five minutes, have kids form pairs. Encourage partners to pray their prayers of thanksgiving together. Finish your meeting by leading kids in singing "Ha-La-La-La" or a song you sang earlier.

TIME STRETCHER

Snack Time

Say: **It's snack time. I've brought a special treat for your snack. I hope you enjoy it.** Give each child a soda cracker. When kids finish eating the crackers, say: **I have another snack for you.** Give each child a large pinch of Pop Rocks or a glass of soda or carbonated water. Ask:

- **In what ways is God like the soda crackers?**
- **In what ways is God like the Pop Rocks** [or soda]**?**
- **What is your favorite thing about God?**

Say: **God is like soda crackers because he's good for us. God gives life to us and helps us grow. God is also like the Pop Rocks** [or soda]**. God is fun and alive, and he wants us to have joy. Our God is so wonderful. He is powerful, caring, and fun—all at the same time.**

God Is Good

THE
POINT
· · · · · · ·
God is good.

HOW TO USE THIS WORSHIP SESSION

Use this session to help kids actively reflect upon the goodness of God.

OBJECTIVES

Kids will
● explore the meaning of God's goodness,
● have an opportunity to praise God for his goodness, and
● tell how they'll reflect God's goodness in their lives.

YOU'LL NEED

● Bibles
● white and gold streamers
● masking tape
● a marker
● an index card for each child
● a cassette or CD player
● *Group's Singable Songs for Children's Ministry* cassette or CD
● one small magnet for each child
● a newsprint flip chart and easel
● a large picture of a church
● a large picture of Jesus or a cross
● snacks such as juice and small bags of peanuts or pretzels
● a trash bag
● *Group's Singable Songs for Children's Ministry* (See index on pp. 121-122.)

BIBLE BASIS

Psalms 34:8; 52:9; 86:5; 92:15; 136:1; Habakkuk 1:13; and James 4:7-8

Several passages from the book of Psalms give insight into God's goodness. God's goodness means more than good behavior. God is good and righteous and pure. God is the source of all goodness; there is no good apart from God. All God does and decrees is good. It's impossible for God to do evil and to consort with evil.

Habakkuk 1:13 says God's eyes are too good to look at evil. James 4:7-8 says we are to flee from evil and draw near to God. When we draw near to God, God will draw near to us.

When we draw near to God and praise and thank him for his goodness, we feel good and are enabled, through God's power, to begin to emulate his goodness. This session will help kids discover more about God's goodness. They'll celebrate and praise God for the goodness he shows to them in their lives.

UNDERSTANDING YOUR KIDS

Kids love to have fun adventures—and there are few things more fun and adventurous for kids than an airplane ride. You'll decorate your meeting area as an airplane and offer kids the chance to learn about God's goodness in a unique environment.

Kids experience God's goodness. But in the busyness of our everyday lives, we seldom have time to sit and reflect on God's goodness and just what it means to us. As Christian teachers, you'll give kids time to sit back, relax, and reflect on God's goodness. You'll give them time to praise and thank God for his goodness. You'll give them a chance to think of ways to reflect God's goodness from their lives to others.

Have an enjoyable flight.

Meeting Area Setup

Set up chairs to resemble the interior of an airplane—two rows of two chairs, each row parallel to the other, with an aisle down the middle. If you have a large group, use a jumbo-jet model for setting up your meeting area. Set up one double row of chairs, then an aisle, one row of chairs five across, then an aisle, and then another double row of chairs.

XX XX

XX XX

XX XX

XX XX

Place a Bible underneath each chair. Use the white and gold streamers to make an "on ramp" for loading and to define the exterior of the aircraft. Use masking tape to mark seat numbers: 1A, 1B, 1C, 1D, 2A, 2B, 2C, 2D, and so on. Use index cards as "boarding passes," and mark the boarding passes ahead of time to correspond with seat numbers.

Dress as a flight attendant for this lesson. For example, wear a navy blue suit or a skirt with a white shirt or blouse. Or if there are people who work for an airline in your church community, ask them to wear their uniforms and help during this session.

XX XXXX XX

XX XXXX XX

XX XXXX XX

During the lesson, kids will hear the "captain" speaking. You can either prerecord the voice or have someone stand behind a screen or in the back of the meeting area and speak loudly or into a microphone. A reproducible script for the captain's part is found on the "Captain Speaks" handout (p. 69).

PRAISE

Prepare for Takeoff

As kids arrive, write their names on boarding passes—one name per pass. Distribute passes to kids. Welcome kids to the "God Is Good" Airline, and board them from the rear of the aircraft. While they're finding their assigned seats, play music from *Group's Singable Songs for Children's Ministry* cassette or CD.

When kids are seated, say: **Welcome to the "God Is Good" Airline. During our time today, you'll travel on our airplane and learn about God's goodness. Turn to your seat partner, say your name, and share one thing you're looking forward to in the next hour.** Pause while kids do this. Say: **Let's get ready for our flight and praise God for his goodness by singing a song.** Sing this song to the tune of "Rock Around the Clock."

> **God is great,**
> **God is good,**
> **And we thank him for this flight.**
> **We're gonna thank him in the morning, noon, and night.**
> **We're gonna thank him 'cause he's outta sight.**
> **Amen, ch-ch-ch-ch-ch-ch-ch-ch.**
> **Amen, ch-ch-ch-ch-ch-ch-ch-ch.**
> **Amen, yeah-h-h-h!**

Teach the song and sing it once; then have kids stand and do the "twist" while they sing it a second time.

Say: **While the aircraft is being prepared for takeoff, we have a moment to think about God's goodness. On behalf of the "God Is Good" Airline, we have a preflight gift for each of you as a thank you for flying our airline.**

Pass one magnet to each child. Say: **Turn to your seat partner and play with the magnets. See what you can discover about them. See what they pick up or attract. Then hold your two magnets together and see what you discover.**

Allow one minute for kids to work with the magnets. Ask:

● **What things did your magnet attract or draw to itself?**

● **What happened when you held two magnets together?**

Read aloud Psalms 86:5 and 136:1. Then ask:

● **What do these verses say about God?**

Read aloud Habakkuk 1:13. Ask:

● **What can't God look at?**

Read aloud James 4:7-8. Ask:

● **What do these verses tell us we should do?**

● **How is drawing near to God and running from evil like some of the discoveries you made about the magnet?**

● **What else can you say about God's goodness?**

Say: **Wow. What a lot of discoveries we made about God's**

goodness. **God is all things good. There is nothing evil or bad in God. Place your magnet under your seat. You'll get to take it with you to your next destination after our flight is over. Let's sing some other songs and praise God for his goodness.**

Sing "What a Mighty God We Serve" and "God's Not Dead" *(Group's Singable Songs for Children's Ministry).*

After you finish singing, say: **Please fold your hands, bow your heads, and join me in a preflight prayer. Dear God, we thank you for your goodness. Help us run from bad things and always draw close to you. You are good. There is nothing bad in you. Help us learn more about your great goodness. Amen.**

POINT

Fasten Your Seat Belts

Say: **Ladies and gentlemen, we are now ready for takeoff on the "God Is Good" Airline. Please remain in your seat while the seat belt sign is on. In case of an emergency, drop to your knees and access the convenient Bible under your seat. The answer to every emergency can be found within its pages. Now sit back and relax as we prepare for takeoff.**

After takeoff, play the recording of the captain's voice saying, "Ladies and gentlemen, this is the captain speaking. Takeoff was perfect, and we're cruising at an altitude of twenty-seven thousand feet. It looks like we'll have a good flight on 'God Is Good' Airline. You'll notice we've turned off the seat belt sign [flip the page of the chart over], so you may get up and move about the cabin if necessary. For now, I'd like you to please stand up. Turn to at least three people close by you, shake their hands, tell them your name, and say one way you noticed God's goodness as you came to church today. For example, you may have noticed the creation around you, the weather, our church, or other things God's given us. Go ahead and share." Pause the tape while kids do this.

Play the tape again to hear the captain say, "If you look out the left side of the aircraft, you'll see one of the ways God shows his goodness to us today." Pause the tape.

Have a helper run down the left side of the aircraft holding a large picture of a church.

Say: **Turn to your seat partner, and answer this question:**
● **How does God show his goodness through our church?**

Give kids a moment to discuss, and then say: **Let's hear some of your answers.** Give kids a chance to respond. Then play the tape to hear the captain's voice saying, "If you look out the right side of the aircraft, you'll see another way God shows his goodness to us." Turn off the tape.

P O I N T

TEACHER TIP

Make a seat belt sign on the first page of a flip chart. When you want the seat belt sign off, flip the first page over.

TEACHER TIP

If you have extra time, play a recording of a plane taking off. Get this from a sound effects cassette tape or CD from your public library.

Have a helper run down the right side of the aircraft holding a large picture of Jesus or a cross.

Say: **Turn to your seat partner and answer these questions:**
● **How does God show his goodness this way?**
● **What did some of you discover about God's goodness?**

Say: **What a lot of ideas about God's goodness. To continue our discussion, we were going to show an in-flight movie. However, we forgot it. We apologize for the inconvenience. But we will have in-flight entertainment. You'll have the chance to work with fellow passengers to learn more about God's goodness.**

In-Flight Entertainment

Have kids form small groups of four to five children. Be sure an older child is in each group. Give each group one of the following Bible passages that speaks to the goodness of God: Psalms 34:8; 92:15; and Matthew 19:17. You can assign the same passage to more than one group.

Say: **Read the Bible verse and discuss in your groups what it says about God's goodness. When you finish, decide on motions and facial expressions you could use to express the meaning of the verse to the rest of the passengers. For example, if you wanted to express "God" you could point up; if you wanted to say something was wrong, you might shake your head "no."** Have kids work in their groups to discover their passage's message. Give kids a few minutes to complete the assignment using the Bibles placed under their seats. Then, one at a time, have groups demonstrate their passages. Have the rest of the passengers try to guess the message. After several guesses, have an older student in each group read the Scripture aloud. If kids didn't guess what the motions represented, have the group explain them.

Food Service

After in-flight presentations, have the passengers give themselves a round of applause for a job well-done. Say: **One of the Bible verses told us to taste and see how good the Lord is. This reminds me that it's time for the "God Is Good" Airline food service.**

Serve snacks such as juice and small bags of peanuts or pretzels.

TEACHER TIP

For a large group, divide the aircraft into four sections. Do this by row and seat numbers. Include four to five of the small groups in each section. Have each group in each section act out their passages for the other groups in their sections. All four sections should complete this activity simultaneously.

PRAYER

Throw It Away

While kids are enjoying their snacks or after they finish (depending on how much time you have), start your prayer time by asking:

● **If God is good and does good things for us, what does that say about how we should act?**

● **Do our actions always show that we believe and love a God who is good? Why or why not?**

● **What keeps us from showing others God's goodness and all the good things he's given us?**

Say: **Anger, worry, feeling sorry for ourselves, and other junk in our lives gets in the way of our being good and our continued thankfulness for God's goodness. It's kind of like how the trash you're holding from snack time gets in the way of our continuing this session. In a moment, I'll come down the aisle with a trash bag. Toss your trash in the bag and say aloud or silently one thing you need to get rid of so you can focus on or reflect God's goodness. For example, toss in your trash and say, "My fear" or "My worries."**

Go down the aisle and collect the trash in a trash bag.

Goodness Prayers

After you're done collecting the trash, read aloud Psalm 52:9. Say: **God, I will thank you forever for what you have done. With those who worship you, I will trust you because you are good. Amen.**

Because God is good, he helps us reflect that goodness to others. Let's remember the verses we talked about earlier in our flight. Ask:

● **What did the verses say about the ways God shows his goodness to us?**

● **How can we show God's goodness to others in our everyday lives?**

Say: **Let's stand and join hands across the aisle and come in for a landing with an all-passenger, one- or two-word prayer. Think of one way you'll show God's goodness to others. When it's your turn, say one or two words such as "Love others," "Forgive," "Be kind," or "Don't fight." I'll start the prayer, and then we'll go to the person next to me and across the aisle until everyone has had a chance to say one or two words aloud. If you want to pass, squeeze the hand of the next person so he or she will know to go ahead and not wait for you. Let's pray. Dear God, you are so good. Thank you for forgiving us when we forget to thank you. Help us be like you and reflect your goodness by doing these things...**

TEACHER TIP

For a large group, the following prayer time will be more effective if you use the section groups from the previous small-group activity.

TEACHER TIP

Have kids tape their magnets to their boarding passes and keep them as reminders of God's goodness in their lives.

After kids have added their words, say "amen" together. Then flip the seat belt sign so kids can see it again. Have kids be seated. Say: **Ladies and gentlemen, you may have noticed that our captain has once again turned on the seat belt sign. We'll be landing soon to head back into our everyday lives. Remember the adventure we had today discovering more about God's goodness. And now, as we make our final approach to the airport, let me remind you to stay in your seats until the plane has arrived at the gate and the captain has turned off the seat belt sign. For information on connecting flights, please refer to your church bulletin, where you'll find information on how you can continue learning more about God's goodness.** Turn on the tape to hear the captain say, "Ladies and gentlemen, thank you for flying 'God Is Good' Airline. We hope your trip was a pleasant one. God bless your day."

TIME STRETCHERS

Good Things

Have kids brainstorm about things they're thankful for and that show the goodness of God to them such as family, friends, animals, food, church, and so on. Have kids sing the following words to the tune of "Row, Row, Row Your Boat":

God, God, you are so good,
And we thank you for...
[Have kids add things they're thankful for.]
God, you are so good.

Design a Logo

Have kids form groups of no more than four. Give each group a sheet of poster board, markers, gold and white streamers, stickers, glitter, and glue. Have groups design logos for the "God Is Good" Airline.

Goodness Hunt

Encourage kids to look for signs of God's goodness during the upcoming week and be ready to share what they found the next time they meet.

THE CAPTAIN SPEAKS

Ladies and gentlemen, this is the captain speaking. Takeoff was perfect, and we're cruising at an altitude of twenty-seven thousand feet. It looks like we'll have a good flight on "God Is Good" Airline. You'll notice we've turned off the seat belt sign, so you may get up and move about the cabin if necessary. For now, I'd like you to please stand up. Turn to at least three people close by you, shake their hands, tell them your name, and say one way you noticed God's goodness as you came to church today. For example, you may have noticed the creation around you, the weather, our church, or other things God's given us. Go ahead and share.

If you look out the left side of the aircraft, you'll see one of the ways God shows his goodness to us today.

If you look out the right side of the aircraft, you'll see another way God shows his goodness to us.

Ladies and gentlemen, thank you for flying "God Is Good" Airline. We hope your trip was a pleasant one. God bless your day.

Special
. . . . .
Days

Palm Sunday: God Is Our King

HOW TO USE THIS WORSHIP SESSION

Use this session on Palm Sunday or any time you want your kids to reflect on the majesty of God.

OBJECTIVES

Kids will
- prepare for Jesus' arrival like the first Palm Sunday crowd,
- experience being a king or queen, and
- discover ways God can be king of their lives.

YOU'LL NEED

- a Bible
- pieces of green construction paper with the design of a palm leaf drawn on them
- scissors
- a sign that reads "Throne"
- a "crown" for a king or queen
- masking tape
- newsprint
- markers
- *Group's Singable Songs for Children's Ministry* (See index on pp. 121-122.)

BIBLE BASIS

Psalm 95:1-7 and Mark 11:1-10

The image of "king" has powerful Old Testament roots. The Israelites lived in a culture in which kings ruled. That person could rule with absolute authority. The king held life and death in his hands. With that cultural background, what did it mean for Israel to confess that the "Lord is the great God, the great King above all gods" (Psalm 95:3)?

The conflict is apparent. Earthly kingdoms are established and ruled by earthly kings. But Israel believed that God was the only king of heaven and earth. When the people of Israel refused to bow

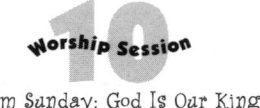

down before an earthly king, they faced ridicule, banishment, and even death. Surely God would intervene in history to bring them a new king from David's line that would rule forever.

Military, conquering kings rode on horses, and people prepared the way before them by throwing their garments on the ground. The Jewish people of Jesus' day expected a conquering, mighty hero. Instead, the Messiah came riding into Jerusalem, bringing his Father's kingdom, on a donkey (Mark 11:1-10).

The people who gathered praised and celebrated his coming. They threw palm branches and even their coats on the road before him. The King had come in his glory. But it was not the earthly kingdom that many were expecting. Jesus rode into Jerusalem as the king of hearts.

UNDERSTANDING YOUR KIDS

Children love to dress up and play being a king or a queen. They don't have the cultural heritage of Europe where kings and queens were granted the power of gods. A child in our culture sees the world of kings and queens as make-believe. It's often hard for children to understand the kingly nature of God's rule.

Palm Sunday is a fun day in the life of the church. Many kids are involved in "palm waving" activities as part of a worship processional. Those palm branches become the symbol of celebration as we welcome the coming of Jesus the king to Jerusalem. Lost in the joy of the moment is the reality that he will soon die for us at the hands of misguided people.

Earthly kings were worshiped, and people followed their laws. Kings lived extravagant lives at the expense of the poor. They stood above and beyond everyone. Jesus was so different. He called everyone to worship his Father in heaven, and he demanded that his followers be faithful to God's laws. He lived humbly and in poverty. Jesus' idea of the kingdom is in sharp contrast to our pictures of earthly kingdoms.

Children can have fun with Palm Sunday. In this worship session, help them see what it means to be part of God's kingdom. There have been many earthly kings. Yet God alone is king of the earth. Through God, we help kids learn the meaning of true royalty. It is only through Jesus that our children can experience God's kingdom on earth and in heaven.

PRAISE

Palm Praise

Welcome kids, and ask:
- **Today is Palm Sunday. What happened on Palm Sunday?**

- **What do you like most about this day?**
- **What do you think the word "king" means?**
- **What do you think you would do if you were a king or queen?**

Say: **In Jesus' time when a king came to visit a city, he rode a horse like a mighty military conqueror. Jesus rode into Jerusalem on a donkey. Jesus came as a different kind of king, a king of peace.**

Gather children around the tables, and set out the green construction paper and scissors. Have kids cut out the palm branches drawn on the construction paper. Ask older kids to help younger ones with the project.

When kids finish, gather in a group and sing "King of Kings" (*Group's Singable Songs for Children's Ministry*). As kids sing this song, have them create celebratory motions. Have them move to the music and wave their palm branches.

When the song is over, ask the children to repeat this phrase: *Jesus, you are king of kings and Lord of lords.* Tell kids they will say the phrase at special times when you pause during a prayer. Invite them to pray with you: **Dear God, thank you for bringing Jesus to Jerusalem.** Encourage children to respond by saying, "Jesus, you are king of kings and Lord of lords." **There was a crowd waiting for him that day.** Have children respond. **The people were so excited to see Jesus coming to their city.** Have children respond. **We're excited today, too.** Have children respond. **Be with us as we learn more about Jesus and Palm Sunday.** Have children respond. Collect the palm branches for use in a later activity.

POINT

Let's Get Ready.

Before the session, mess up the area where you usually meet so kids notice that it needs cleaning. If they ask you about it during the "Praise" section time, tell them you'll talk with them about it later. Ask:

- **What did you notice about our meeting area when you arrived today?**
- **What do you think we can do about it?**

Say: **You know that's a great idea. That's probably what happened when people realized Jesus was coming to visit Jerusalem. They needed to get everything ready for his arrival. Let's get our meeting area ready for Jesus.**

Have kids form small groups, and assign the groups specific projects: straightening chairs, moving tables, cleaning up paper, and so on. When the room is cleaned up, gather everyone together in a circle. Ask:

TEACHER TIP

If you have a very large group or use a meeting area that is not conducive to this activity, do the following activity instead. Have kids form groups of six to eight. If possible, have adult volunteers sit with each group. Say: Pretend someone very famous is coming to your house to visit. What kinds of things would you do to get ready for this visit? In your groups, talk about what you would do. After kids have had a chance to discuss, ask them to gather again as a large group, and ask the last question from the original activity.

● **What does our meeting area look like now?**

● **How did you feel while you were helping to clean things up?**

● **What do you think the people who met Jesus on Palm Sunday were thinking or feeling after they had gotten ready for him?**

Read aloud Mark 11:1-10. Say: **It sounds like that was a very special day. I think lots of kids were there on the road to see Jesus. You know, Jesus really liked children. I think he waved at every one of them that day. Wow, what would you have thought if you had been there and Jesus had waved at you?** Pause for answers. **Sometimes we aren't ready for Jesus. Sometimes we get really busy and don't have time for him. Sometimes we forget he's even around. Sometimes we think we don't need him at all. That's not a very good way to treat a king.**

Royalty for a Day

TEACHER TIP

If you have a large group, have kids form four groups of equal size for this activity. Have an adult volunteer conduct this activity with each group. Have kids stay in these groups for the discussion time. Ask your adult helpers to lead the discussion.

Tell the kids that some of them are going to have a chance to play a king or queen. The rest of the group will be the servants of the king or queen. Put a chair in the center of the group, and place the "Throne" sign on it. Pick out several children of different ages, and tell them they're going to be a king or a queen. One at a time, let each child sit on the throne. Place a crown on each child before he or she sits down.

Say: **You get to be king or queen over the group. When you're sitting in the throne, you can make the group members do anything you want them to do. They must follow every order you give. You can't ask them to do something that might injure someone or ask them to use ugly words. Other than that, you can make them say or do anything you want. For example, you might say, "I want everyone to kneel down" or "I want everyone to stand on one foot" or "I want everyone to walk around in a circle." You get the idea.** Pick an older child to be the first king or queen. Then follow with a few others. Not everyone will have a chance to be the king or queen. That's part of the learning experience.

When a few kids have had a chance to be a king or a queen, gather the group in a circle. Ask:

● **How did it feel taking orders from a king or queen?**

● **How did it feel being the king or the queen and having power over the group?**

● **How did you feel when you weren't chosen to be the king or queen?**

● **What would you have done if you had been king or queen?**

● **What did you like or not like about what the kings and queens did?**

● **What do you think Jesus would have done differently if he**

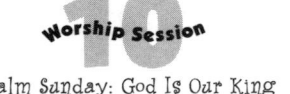

had been the king giving the orders?

Say: **Being a king or queen is a tough job. Some of you made the group do hard things. It looked like you enjoyed having the power.** Ask:

● **What would Jesus want you to do as kings or queens?**

Say: **Here's something from one of the psalms in the Bible that might help us understand more about how God is our king.** Read aloud Psalm 95:1-7, and then say: **It says we should worship God and kneel before him because he is the only king. We're God's people, and God loves us. God is a mighty king, and he'll always protect us. Everything that was made belongs to God. Even us. Only God can be king. God sent Jesus to help us know what kind of king God really is. God loved us so much he would even let his Son, Jesus, die for us. God made us part of his royal family because of Jesus. We have a special place before God when we believe in Jesus. God is king.**

Who Do We Worship?

Gather kids together in a circle. Place the crown that you used during the previous activity in the center of the group. Ask for a volunteer from the older kids to stand in the center of the group. Pick up the crown, and put it on his or her head. Ask the kids to kneel down, wave their arms up and down, and say, "We praise you, [name of child], oh mighty king [or queen]." Let each person in the circle take a turn wearing the crown. Repeat the activity with each child who wears the crown. Ask:

● **How did it feel when you were wearing the crown and everyone was bowing down to you?**

● **How did it feel when you had to bow down to the person who was the king or queen?**

● **How was this experience like the way some people treat us?**

● **How do you think this experience was the same or different from the way Jesus entered Jerusalem?**

Say: **Jesus didn't want to be an earthly king who ruled over people. Jesus wanted to be the king of people's hearts. He wanted to bring people together so they would find God again. He didn't want people worshiping him as we just worshiped the king or queen. That wasn't real worship. He wanted people to worship his Father in heaven because they loved him and knew he was the king of the world.**

TEACHER TIP

If you used the large-group strategy suggested in the last activity, continue to have kids remain in those groups for this activity.

PRAYER

Palm Prayers

Make a large circle on the floor of your meeting area with masking tape. The size will depend on the size of your group. On a sheet of newsprint, write, "God, I want you to be king of my life and help me..." Display the newsprint where kids can see it.

Retrieve the palm leaves the kids used during the "Praise" section. Have kids form multi-age groups of three or four. Give each child a palm leaf and a marker. Say: **God wants to be king over our lives. Talk in your groups about what that means for each of you. Complete this statement, and write or draw your answers on your palm leaves: "God, I want you to be king of my life and help me..." For example, you might write, "be a better friend" or "love my parents more" or "be nicer to my little sister." Think about all the ways you can let God be king of your life. The older kids can help the younger kids with their ideas. When you finish, take your palm leaves and lay them in the circle on the floor.**

When the groups complete their work, have everyone stand around the outside of the circle. Have kids march around the palm leaf circle and chant together, "Hosanna! Blessed is he who comes in the name of the Lord" (Mark 11:9).

After the kids march around the circle several times, stop the group and ask them to hold hands. Pray: **Dear God, thank you for Palm Sunday. Thank you giving us Jesus. Help us make you king of our lives. Help us turn to you all the time. Help us remember that you are our king. Thank you for loving us so much. In Jesus' name we pray, amen.** Allow kids to take home their palm leaves as reminders of the meaning of Palm Sunday and as reminders that God is king.

TIME STRETCHER

Palm Sunday Puppets

Have kids form pairs that consist of one younger child and one older child. Give each pair a paper lunch sack. Provide construction paper, scissors, yarn, tape, glue sticks, and markers. Assign the pairs one of the following people to make into a puppet:

- Jesus,
- a disciple,
- a donkey,
- a woman,
- a man, and
- a child.

If some kids finish earlier than others, they can make another puppet. When groups finish their work, read the story in Mark 11 again. Ask pairs to act out the story with their puppets.

If you have a large group of kids, have them form groups of six. Have each group make all six puppets and plan their own puppet show.

Easter: God Is Forever

THE POINT

God will always live.

HOW TO USE THIS WORSHIP SESSION

Use this session at Easter or any time you want to celebrate life.

OBJECTIVES

Kids will

● celebrate the good news of Easter,

● experience ways God is always with them, and

● thank God for always being there.

YOU'LL NEED

● a Bible

● three signs reading, "Sorry, He's Not Here!"

● cupcakes

● regular birthday candles and special birthday candles that re-light after they're blown out (You can find these candles in the party-supply sections of most stores.)

● matches

● a bowl of water

● a smooth pebble or rock for each child (Rocks should be big enough to write the word "God" on them.)

● thin-line permanent markers

● an empty plastic Easter egg for each child

● scissors

● a photocopy of the "Easter Egg Prayers" handout (p. 87) for each child

● newsprint

● tape

● *Group's Singable Songs for Children's Ministry* (See index on pp. 121-122.)

BIBLE BASIS

Psalm 121 and John 20:1-9

Easter comes crashing upon us with the awesome power of ocean waves breaking against the shore. We're swept away by the almost incomprehensible idea of what God's love has done for us through the resurrection of Jesus Christ. Everything we are as Christians is held together by the impact of Easter. The empty tomb was God's final statement that we are his children, and not even the finality of death is more powerful than faith in our risen Lord.

John 20:1-9 tells us the story of the empty tomb. The first eyes that looked around in that empty tomb were rubbed in disbelief. Who stole Jesus' body? Why would they do that? No, it can't be true. He can't be alive again. Or is he?

Then he came into their presence. They saw his hands, and they experienced his glorious radiance. They heard the promise for all eternity that he would be with them and us. These are ideas so lofty that we barely comprehend them. This is truth so spectacular that we spend a lifetime getting new glimpses into it.

The good news of Easter becomes even more majestic when laid alongside the promises of Psalm 121. The God who kept Israel now keeps us secure in the arms of Jesus. The God who has always been more powerful than any evil now equips us with the ultimate weapon of the lordship of Christ. Yes, God was there in the heart of the psalmist, and God is here in our lives through the Easter message.

UNDERSTANDING YOUR KIDS

Easter is always an exciting time for kids. Many families have Easter traditions that kids eagerly await. Even the local church has special Easter traditions that help us set this day aside as something out of the ordinary.

Children think concretely. They understand Easter in vivid, literal images. They understand that God brought Jesus back to life in a literal way, but from that point on the story gets abstract. What does it mean that Jesus now lives forever with God? What does it mean that Jesus is now always with us? These are abstract ideas that we must be careful with when dealing with the Easter story.

Easter egg hunts, new clothes, Easter baskets, and lots of other distractions can take away from the good news of this day. Children need help experiencing what Easter is about. As we teach them, we must not ignore their questions about Easter. Even when they ask those unanswerable questions, we can still help them deal with the reality of Easter.

God did something incomprehensible. Through God's power, Jesus defeated death. Our faith in Jesus and his resurrection opens the door to heaven. This is big, glorious, abstract stuff that must be put in little understandable bites for kids.

Use this lesson as a celebration of Easter. Watch for teachable moments as children share their questions and make new discoveries.

Easter is here! Jesus is alive! Life is never going to be the same again. Hallelujah! Tell the world.

PRAISE

Easter Excitement

Welcome kids, and wish them a happy Easter. Ask:
- **Why do we celebrate Easter?**
- **What are some ways you celebrate Easter in your family?**
- **What do you like best about church on Easter Sunday?**

Say: **Easter is a very special day. God loves us so much that he wanted his Son, Jesus, to be with us always. Jesus loves his Father in heaven, and Jesus loves us. That's why he was willing to die for us. Some mean people thought they got rid of Jesus by killing him, but God was more powerful. Today everything is different. It's Easter, and Jesus is alive.**

Lead children in singing "Ho-Ho-Ho-Hosanna" (*Group's Singable Songs for Children's Ministry*). Make up hand motions to the song as the children sing.

Next sing "He's Alive" (*Group's Singable Songs for Children's Ministry*). Ask the older children to do the clapping parts and the younger children to sing the words. After they know the song, switch roles and let the older children sing and the younger ones clap.

The Day the Tomb Was Empty

Gather in a standing group, and read aloud John 20:1-9 as follows. Ask kids to do the motions as you read. Make sure kids leave enough space between each other to do the motions. You might want to have a helper mime the motions for kids to follow.

Early on the first day of the week, while it was still dark,	Make stretching motions and yawn.
Mary Magdalene went to the tomb and saw that the stone had been removed from the entrance.	Put your hands on your forehead as if peering into an opening.
So she came running to Simon Peter and the other disciple, the one Jesus loved, and said,	Run in place.
"They have taken the Lord out of the tomb, and we don't know where they have put him!"	Find a partner, put your hands on your partner's shoulders, and gently shake them.

So Peter and the other disciple started for the tomb.	Make a circle with everyone, and quietly run in place.
Both were running, but the other disciple outran Peter and reached the tomb first. He bent over and looked in at the strips of linen lying there but did not go in.	Stop running, and bend over like you are looking into the tomb.
Then Simon Peter, who was behind him, arrived and went into the tomb.	Jump forward.
He saw the strips of linen lying there, as well as the burial cloth that had been around Jesus' head.	Scratch your head like you're wondering about something.
The cloth was folded up by itself, separate from the linen. Finally the other disciple, who had reached the tomb first, also went inside.	Shake hands with a partner.
He saw and believed.	Jump up and down, waving your arms.

Ask children to pray with you: **Dear God, we wonder what Mary Magdalene, Peter, and John thought when they got to the empty tomb. Thank you for bringing Jesus back to life. We thank you that he lives forever. He loves us so much, and now he wants to be our Savior. Help us follow him every day. In Jesus' name we pray, amen.**

POINT

He's Not Here!

Before the session, find three rooms in your church you can use for this activity. In each room, place a large sign that reads, "Sorry, He's Not Here!"

Say: **Wow! What an experience Mary Magdalene, Peter, and John had that morning. Think about it. All three of them went to the tomb and saw that the big rock had rolled away from the entrance. They looked in and found nothing but the special wrappings that had been around Jesus' body. For a while all they could imagine was that someone had stolen Jesus' body. Then they wondered, What if he really has come back to life?**

Tell the children they're going hunting for Jesus just as Mary and Peter and John did. Take children to visit the rooms you chose earlier. If you're in an area of your church where you will not disturb

TEACHER TIP

If your church does not allow you to use extra rooms, perhaps you can designate a special area in your meeting space with the signs or use hallways close to your meeting area.

others, you can let children run ahead once they know which room you're heading to. When you get to each room, ask one child to carry away the sign that reads, "Sorry, He's Not Here!"

After visiting all the empty rooms, go back to your meeting area. Ask:

● **How did you feel each time we got to a room and found the sign telling us Jesus wasn't there?**

● **In what ways was your experience like what happened to Mary Magdalene, Peter, and John?**

Say: **When we go looking for something and don't find it, we have lots of questions. I'm sure Peter and John wondered what had happened to Jesus' body. The Bible says John "saw and believed." That means he knew that Jesus was alive. What a great experience for him. That's what God wants us to feel on Easter morning.**

Curious Candles

Have kids form groups of four to six. An adult needs to be part of each group. Give each group two cupcakes. On one cupcake, put a regular birthday candle; on the other cupcake, the "trick" candle. Tell the group you want to have a party to celebrate Easter. Read aloud Matthew 28:20b. Say: **Jesus told us he would always be with us. Let's celebrate that.** Have the adult in each group light both candles and invite group members to blow them out. Some of the candles will keep relighting after being blown out. Let the children keep trying to blow out the trick candles. Have a bowl of water nearby so you can extinguish the candles. If you want, provide cupcakes for all the kids to eat after this activity.

Gather kids together as a large group, and ask:

● **What happened to the candles?**

● **What were you thinking when you saw some of the candles start burning again?**

● **How was that experience like what God did on Easter morning?**

Say: **People thought they had gotten rid Jesus just as you thought you had blown out your candles. But God had other plans. Some of you didn't know you had special candles on your cupcakes just as people didn't know God had a special plan for Easter. God brought Jesus back to life, and Jesus is always with God now. That means he is always with us. He will never go away again because he told us so in the Bible passage I read.**

Rock-Solid Reminders

Before this activity, set out the rocks and markers.

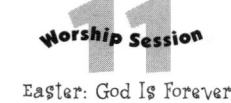

Gather the group around the area where you have set out the smooth rocks and permanent markers. Ask each child to pick a rock. Have kids form small groups so older children are with younger children. Tell them to write "God" on their rocks. Ask older children to help the younger ones.

After kids are finished, gather together in a large group. Read Psalm 121. Say: **That psalm tells us that God is always watching over us and keeping us safe.** Ask:

● **How old do you think your rock is?**

● **How long do you think your rock will last?**

Say: **That rock is older than you or me or our church or even our country. That rock has been here a long, long time. It will be here after we die. God is like that rock. God has always been here. And now God is always with us in Jesus. That's what happened on Easter. Take your rock home and look at it every day. Remember that God has always been here and always will be here just like that rock.**

PRAYER

Easter Egg Prayers

Before the session, cut apart the slips from the "Easter Egg Prayers" handouts (p. 87).

Give each child an empty plastic Easter egg and the phrases from the "Easter Egg Prayers" handouts (p. 87). Say: **I want you to think about how you would complete this statement: God, you are always alive. Thank you for...** Write the phrase on newsprint, and tape the newsprint to a wall where kids can see it. Say: **On your strips of paper are phrases that complete the sentence. Fold up these strips of paper, and put them in your plastic eggs. Then put on the top.** Tell the kids to open their eggs each day next week, take out one of the slips, and read it as a prayer. Younger kids can ask parents to help them read the slips.

Have kids form prayer circles of four to six. Ask kids to go around their circles and close with a prayer during which each child completes this sentence: God, you are always alive. Thank you for...

TIME STRETCHER

Easter Eating

Give kids some 11x17-inch sheets of white construction or drawing paper. Provide crayons, scissors, colored construction paper, glue sticks, and markers. Tell kids to make special place mats celebrating Easter that they can use at mealtimes. Kids should make one place mat for each person in their families. Give kids some examples

TEACHER TIP

To save time if you have a small group of kids, fill each egg with the seven slips of paper prior to the worship session. Then place the eggs in a large basket, and ask the group to sit in a circle around it. Say a prayer together with each person completing this sentence: God, you are always alive. Thank you for... After the group completes the prayer, hand an egg to each child. Tell kids to take the eggs home, pull out one of the slips each day, and read it as a prayer with their families. Young children can have parents help them read the slips.

of what they can put on their place mats—for example, a picture of the empty tomb, the words "Jesus is alive," or flowers and butterflies as symbols of Easter. Ask older children to work with younger children on the project.

Easter Egg Prayers

...making me a special person.

...a beautiful world to live in.

...bringing Jesus back to life.

...good food to make me strong.

...people who love me.

...loving me so much that you sent Jesus to die for me.

...my friends.

Easter: God Is All-Powerful

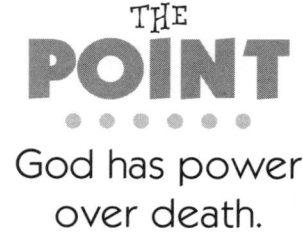

THE POINT

God has power over death.

HOW TO USE THIS WORSHIP SESSION

Use this session at Easter or any time you want your kids to reflect on God's power (specifically power over death).

OBJECTIVES

Kids will
- review the Easter story,
- discover that God's power is available for use in their lives, and
- celebrate God's power.

YOU'LL NEED

- a Bible
- newsprint
- markers
- tape
- pencils
- paper
- photocopies of the "Breaking News" handout (p. 95)
- butcher paper
- construction paper
- scissors
- glue
- glitter
- magazine pictures
- rulers or measuring tape
- *Group's Singable Songs for Children's Ministry* (See index on pp. 121-122.)

BIBLE BASIS

1 Chronicles 29:10-15; Psalm 77:14; Matthew 27:57–28:20; and Ephesians 3:20

Easter is a time we stop to celebrate Jesus' resurrection. But often one would think it was only a time for Easter eggs, new clothes, musical presentations, and gifts. These things are not wrong, but

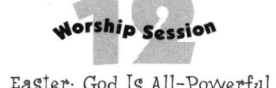

sometimes we get so caught up in the celebration trappings that we forget the all-important Easter message of God's power over death.

1 Chronicles 29:10-15 shows God's people celebrating the majesty of God and his power. This is the same God who raised Jesus from the dead. Psalm 77:14 offers praises for God's power.

The last days of Jesus' earthly ministry are recorded in Matthew 27 and 28. Looking at passages from these chapters helps us walk through the Easter story and see a vivid picture of God's power.

Ephesians 3:20 is a wonderful promise from God about his immeasurable power. When we trust God, he can do far more for us than we could ever believe.

UNDERSTANDING YOUR KIDS

Kids can be confused these days about where true power comes from. But we can help them understand that true and absolute power comes from God. Kids can understand that God's power is available to them in their everyday lives.

Through the Easter story and the demonstration of God's power through the resurrection of Jesus, kids see that the God they follow and worship can do anything. Nothing can stop the power of God.

Use this lesson to help your kids see that the celebration of Easter is more than just chocolate bunnies and new clothes. Help kids see it as the basis of our relationship with God and an incredible picture of the power of God.

PRAISE

Powerful Praising

Welcome kids to your Easter celebration, and lead them in singing "God's Not Dead" *(Group's Singable Songs for Children's Ministry)*. Sing the song a few times, teaching kids the hand motions found in the leaders guide. After you finish singing, have kids form multi-age groups of four. Ask the groups to answer the following questions:

● **How can you feel God in your everyday lives?**

● **Even though we can't really see God, how do you know he's with you?**

● **How do we know that God's not dead?**

Gather kids together in a large group, and ask them to share some of their answers to the questions. Say: **You did a great job singing that song. Today we're celebrating Easter. What comes to your mind when you think of Easter?** Give kids time to respond, and say: **Easter shows us that Jesus had the power to defeat death. The most important thing about Easter is that Jesus is alive again. Because of that, we have the opportunity to live forever**

> **TEACHER TIP**
>
> If you have a large group of kids, make your groups larger. Kids can form groups of six to eight.

POINT

with him. **Not only can we live forever, but when we put our faith in Jesus, we have God's power with us while we live on earth. We have God's power to help us live every day.**

Lead kids in singing "He's Alive" *(Group's Singable Songs for Children's Ministry).* Say: **We've been singing about Jesus being alive. Let's talk about some ways we know that Jesus is alive.** Allow time for kids to respond, and write their responses on a piece of newsprint that's taped to a wall.

Say: **Wow. There are lots of ways we know Jesus is alive today.** Lead kids in a short prayer, praising God for using his power to raise Jesus from the dead.

Say: **When we praise God, we're telling God how much we love him and appreciate what he does for us. Today we're praising God for raising Jesus from the dead and for being all-powerful. That power is so great that God can do anything. What are some ways we can praise God for his power?** Allow time for kids to respond, and then say: **We can praise God by praying or by singing songs. Sometimes we sing fast songs of praise, and other times we praise God by singing songs that are more like prayers. Let's sing a worshipful song to praise God for his power.** Sing "Awesome God" *(Group's Singable Songs for Children's Ministry)* a few times, and then lead the group in a prayer. Pray: **God, we thank you for your power that you have given to us through Jesus. Thank you for Jesus and what he did for us when he died on the cross. Thank you for bringing him alive again so we can live forever with you. In Jesus' name, amen.**

What's Easter All About?

Have kids re-form their groups from the earlier activity. Give each group a pencil and a piece of paper. Say: **Pretend someone who has never heard of Easter asks you to explain what it is. Take a few minutes to write down what your group would tell this person.** Give groups five minutes to discuss their answers. Then have a reader from each group read the group's answer. End this activity by thanking God for giving us a reason to celebrate Easter.

POINT

The Evening News

Say: **Repeat after me: He's alive.** Wait for kids to respond. **Now let's say it again—only a little louder.** Wait for kids to respond. **Really loudly.** Wait for kids to respond. **That was great. Jesus is alive because he has the power to defeat death. Now we're going to look at what the Bible says about Jesus rising from the dead.** Have the group form three multi-age groups. Give each group one of

the following Bible passages: Matthew 27:57-65; 28:1-10; and 28:11-20. Give each group a photocopy of the "Breaking News" handout (p. 95), pencils, and a Bible. Say: **As you read these Bible verses, I want you to pretend your group is a team for a television news show. Your job is to report to the public what was happening in the life of Jesus in your verses. Several of you might want to be reporters. Some of you can be reporting from the scene, or you can be in the newsroom reporting the story. Some of you can pretend to be the camera operators or the director of the news program. You decide how to tell the story just like you are real reporters. To help prepare your news reports, try to answer the six questions listed on the handout about your part of the story. Who are the people involved in the story? What happened? When did the story happen? Where did the story take place? Why did these events happen? How did these events happen?** Give groups time to prepare their presentations. When groups are finished, have each group present its report to the large group.

After the presentations, ask:

● **Where was Jesus buried? What kind of precautions did the government take around his burial place? Why?**

● **Who went to see Jesus' tomb? What did they find when they got there?**

● **Who did Jesus appear to after he rose from the dead? How did they react?**

● **If you had been one of the people Jesus appeared to, how do you think you would've reacted?**

Say: **People found it hard to believe that Jesus wasn't dead anymore. But he's alive, and soon they came to realize it was true. Jesus is alive again. He's defeated death. He's shown the world God's power. That's what we celebrate on Easter. Now let's look at some other verses from the Bible to discover more about God's power, God's ability to do anything, and how we can praise God for that power.**

Points of Power

Have kids return to their groups from the previous activity and look up and discuss the following Old Testament passages: 1 Chronicles 29:10-15 and Psalm 77:14. As they read the passages, ask them to discuss the following questions. You may want to write the questions on newsprint, a dry-erase board, or an overhead transparency ahead of time. Ask:

● **What are some things you think are powerful? What makes them powerful?**

● **What are some words used in these Bible passages to describe God's power?**

TEACHER TIP

If you have a large group and had to form more than three groups, have an adult helper or helpers take the other groups to another part of your meeting area to present their reports.

● **Describe what you think God's power is like.**

After kids finish, bring them back together in the large group, and have them share some of their answers.

Powerful Pictures

Direct kids to supplies such as butcher paper, construction paper, scissors, glue, glitter, magazine pictures, and markers you have set out beforehand. Say: **Now that we've explored God's power over death and some other ways God is powerful, we're going to make collages that represent God's power. A collage is a collection of pictures or drawings that has a theme. For example, you might glue a picture of an airplane on your paper because even though an airplane has lots of power, God has more. Or you can write words about God's power to go with your pictures.** As kids work on their projects, circulate among them, asking them about the images they chose and how the images remind them of God's absolute power. After kids finish, say: **When we finish today, remember to take your collages home. Hang them somewhere where you can see them every day and be reminded of how powerful God is.**

PRAYER

Getting to Know Jesus

Say: **On Easter we celebrate Jesus' defeat of death. He's alive and will live forever. He wants us to be his friend and have the power to live forever, too. We do this by telling God we believe Jesus is alive, by telling God we love him, and by telling God we're sorry for the bad things we've done. We ask for forgiveness and promise to follow and love Jesus every day. When we do this, we have put our faith in Jesus. When we put our faith in Jesus, we have God's power with us every day to help us. And, like Jesus, we will live forever. Some of you already may have put your faith in Jesus. That's great. But if you haven't and you would like to, all you have to do is tell God you want to put your faith in Jesus. We're going to be quiet for a minute to give you all a chance to talk to God. If you want to talk to him about putting your faith in Jesus, you can do that now.** After kids finish praying, invite anyone who talked with God about putting his or her faith in Jesus to tell you or another adult helper about it after the session is over. Please make sure you talk to the parents of these children. Some children may not be comfortable talking about this decision with you. Make sure they understand that is OK, but let them know they should talk about it with their parents.

TEACHER TIP

If you have a large group of kids, distribute these supplies in various areas of your meeting space. Have the group form smaller age-level groups. For example, send the kindergartners through second-graders to one area and the third- and fourth-graders to another area. Ask an adult helper to work with each group.

TEACHER TIP

This section contains an opportunity for the children to put their faith in Jesus. Please feel free to use it as written or modify the words to suit your particular theological tradition.

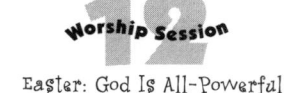

Measuring Power

Have kids form trios. Say: **Let's look at one more verse from the Bible that tells us about God's power.** Read aloud Ephesians 3:20. Ask:

● **What do you think it means when it says God's power is at work within us?**

Give each trio a ruler or measuring tape. Say: **Measure the foot of someone in your group.** Allow time for kids to do this. **Now measure the arm of someone in your group.** Allow time for kids to do this. **Now find a chair, and measure how high it is.** Allow time for kids to do this. **Now measure the length of one of the walls in our meeting area.** Allow kids time to do this. **Now measure the height of one of the walls in our meeting area.** Allow kids time to do this. Some will protest that they can't do it because they aren't tall enough. **Some of you couldn't measure the wall because you weren't tall enough. Now measure the height of our church building.** Kids will protest that they can't do this. **OK, then measure the distance from here to the star in the universe that's the farthest away.** Kids will say they can't do that. **That's right, you can't do it because for you the distance to that star is immeasurable. We can't measure it. That's what the Bible verse says about what God's power can do for us. It's so big and wonderful we can't measure it. But we know it's there because God told us he's powerful, and God's power is shown in raising Jesus from the dead. That power can help you every day in school, with your friends, at home, with any hard things in your life.** Collect the rulers and measuring tape. Have kids gather together in a large group. Say: **I want you to think of one thing in your life in which you need God's power this week. We're going to be really quiet for a few seconds, and during that time, I want you to ask God to use his power to help you this week.** Have a short time of silent prayer. Close the prayer time by thanking God out loud for raising Jesus from the dead and for giving us that power in our lives. End the session by singing "He's Alive" one more time.

TIME STRETCHER

Mo' Power

Have your group form two or three teams. Give each team the name of a Bible character who was given God's power to accomplish something that seemed impossible. For example, you could use the story of David and Goliath, Daniel in the lions' den, or Gideon fighting the battle with few men. You may want to give each team a short synopsis of the Bible character's story. Each team will take

a turn acting out the story of the character while the other teams try to guess who the Bible character is. Have a kitchen timer ready, and allow each team one minute for its presentation.

If you have a large group, have several groups of teams play the game simultaneously in different areas of your meeting space.

Breaking News

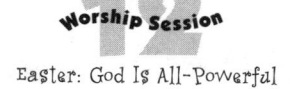

Who are the people involved in the story?

What happened?

When did the story happen?

Where did the story take place?

Why did these events happen?

How did these events happen?

Preparing for Christmas: God Is Faithful

THE POINT

God is faithful to his promises.

HOW TO USE THIS WORSHIP SESSION

Use this session during the Christmas season or when you want kids to reflect on God's faithfulness.

OBJECTIVES

Kids will
- understand God's faithfulness,
- experience anticipation, and
- learn that the birth of Jesus was a much-looked-forward-to event.

YOU'LL NEED

- a Bible
- a box that's wrapped with four layers of gift-wrap and that contains enough candy or small toy items for each child in the class
  - 9x13-inch pink, purple, and white construction paper
  - photocopies of the "Christmas Patterns" handout (p. 103)
  - scissors
  - pencils
  - glue
  - candle "flames" cut from yellow or orange construction paper

BIBLE BASIS

Genesis 12:2; 2 Samuel 7:16; Isaiah 9:6-7; and Luke 2:10-11

Advent is an eagerly anticipated season in the life of every Christian because it's the doorway to that sacred and holy season celebrating the birth of Jesus. This season provides an opportunity for us to focus on and prepare for the celebration of the world-changing occurrence that took place in Bethlehem all those many years ago.

The Old Testament passages in this session show the progression of God's promises to his people, and the verses from Luke tell of the angel announcing the fulfillment of those promises with the birth of Jesus.

Beginning four Sundays before Christmas and culminating with the observance of Christ's birth on Christmas Day, Advent fills us with anticipation and kindles in us a sense of awe for the love God has for us. But we all experience the Christmas "rush." Even when we try to minimize the hustle and bustle of the season, there are still gifts to be exchanged; people to be remembered; cards to be sent; children's plays, concerts, and programs to attend; church activities...whew! In the midst of all this observing, Advent can help us focus for a moment on the wonder of this beautiful story. Observing the symbols of the season with your family is a simple way to focus everyone's thoughts throughout the month before Christmas.

UNDERSTANDING YOUR KIDS

The shopping malls fill with Christmas decorations soon after Halloween. Kids are bombarded with secular Christmas messages earlier and earlier each year. This makes church celebrations of Advent and Christmas all the more important. So first use this worship session as a way to prepare your kids spiritually for the coming Christmas celebration.

Promises are important to kids. What parent hasn't heard the plaintive wail "But you promised" when counted-on plans have gone awry. Promises kept are the way kids learn to trust adults. In the same way, if we want our kids to trust God, we need to show them how he's faithful to keep his promises to them. The season of Advent is a four-week celebration of God's perfect promise-keeping. God said One would come who would bring reconciliation between God and creation. That promise is kept in the gift of Jesus, God incarnate. Use this worship session to teach kids that God is faithful to keep all his promises.

PRAISE

Promises Kept

Say: **In our worship today, we'll learn the meaning of the word "faithful" and how God demonstrates faithfulness to us. I'm going to tell you what I've been doing for the last five days, and I want you to help me. When I stretch my arms as if I'm just waking up, I want you to say with me, "and the sun came up."** Relate events of a five-day period in your life, embellishing the story to make it interesting. End the story of each day by saying: **I spoke with God, said my prayers, and went to sleep.** Have kids respond each time by saying, "and the sun came up." When you finish, say:

● **Tell me something that happened every single day in my life during that five-day period.**

Say: **Something that happens every day is the sunrise. The sun comes up every day as it has for thousands of years. It came up every day for Abraham, David, and Isaiah in the Old Testament. It came up and shone on Jesus after his birth, and it's risen every day and shone on everyone since then. Sometimes we can't see it when it's cloudy and the rain spills down, but if we were tall enough to see above the clouds, we'd see the faithful, old sun. And just as we can count on the sun in the sky every day, we can also count on God's love and care for us in our lives. God's promised to take care of us, and God is faithful. What are some other places where God shows his faithfulness to us in our everyday lives?** Spark kids' thinking about seasonal changes with hints about new leaves on the trees in the spring, flowers and vegetables that grow in the summer, and leaves turning colors in the fall. Explain that God faithfully provides these things for us so we can live on this planet.

Teach the first verse and chorus of the old hymn "Great Is Thy Faithfulness." Explain the meaning behind some of the old-fashioned words. Emphasize the phrase "Thou changest not, thy compassions, they fail not; as Thou hast been Thou forever wilt be." You may want to refer to the discussion you had about the sun coming up every day to illustrate the unchanging nature of God. If you have time, teach the second verse.

Say: **We're entering the season known as Advent, which is that time when we look forward to the coming of Christmas. But Christmas takes so long to get here. Advent begins on four Sundays before Christmas and helps us prepare to celebrate the birth of our Savior, Jesus. Advent also serves to remind us that God made a promise to his people many years ago that he would send a Savior. God was faithful to keep that promise when he sent Jesus into the world.** Ask kids to define "promise." Make sure they know that a promise is when you give your word that you'll do something and you won't let anything stop you from keeping your promise. Say: **When the news finally came that God fulfilled his promise and Jesus was born, imagine the great joy felt by all of God's people. Let's sing a Christmas song that expresses that feeling of joy at the Savior's birth.**

Have kids sing the first verse of "Joy to the World."

POINT

What's in the Box?

Have the kids gather in a circle on the floor. Before you begin this

TEACHER TIP

For a large group, adapt this activity in the following ways: Have the group form small circles. Have a wrapped package for each circle, and tell the story to the whole group as adult helpers work with each circle. Or set the package in the front of the room where all the kids can see it. Tell the story to the large group, inviting kids up to unwrap the package at the various pauses in the story.

section of the session, conduct a quick review about the Bible to remind the kids that the Bible is divided into two parts: the Old Testament and the New Testament. The Old Testament is the history of God's people prior to the coming of Jesus and contains many promises pointing to the birth of a Savior for God's people. Explain that the New Testament begins with the birth of Jesus.

Then say: **As Christians, we celebrate the birth of our Savior, Jesus, at Christmastime.** Ask:

● **What makes it so hard to wait for Christmas?**

Ask kids to name some of their favorite things about Christmas. When you hear answers ranging from presents to food, from family to twinkling lights, you'll feel the excitement build among the kids.

Show kids the wrapped gift. Pass it to the child next to you. Say: **We'll pass this gift around the circle. Each of you will have a chance to hold it and shake it.** After each child has a chance to hold the gift, place the package in the center of the circle. Tell kids that there's a surprise in the package for each of them but that they must be patient while you tell them a story about how Christmas came about.

Say: **Back in Old Testament times there was no Christmas to celebrate. Jesus hadn't been born yet. But God told people for years that one day a child would be born who would grow up to be the Savior of any person who would put faith in him.** Pause, and ask one of the kids to unwrap the first layer of the gift and then place the gift back in the center of the circle.

Then say: **Way, way back in the Old Testament in the very first book of the Bible, there was a man who loved God, who prayed often, and who listened to what God had to say to him. He had a wife named Sarah, and when he was old, he had a son named Isaac. Can anybody tell me what the man's name was?** Pause for a response. **His name was Abraham, and God loved him very much. God made a promise to Abraham, saying many special opportunities would come his way.** Read aloud Genesis 12:2. Say: **In this passage, God says he will provide someone to save all people and that the person will come from Abraham's family. Abraham was honored that God thought so highly of him, but he knew the promised Savior would not come for many years.** Pause, and ask another child to unwrap the next layer of the gift.

Many years later, in the book of 2 Samuel which is also in the Old Testament, God made a similar promise to David, who was a descendant of Abraham's. Read aloud 2 Samuel 7:16. Say: **David was happy that God was pleased with him and glad the promised Savior would be a part of his family. He must have waited anxiously for this child to be born, but it didn't happen in his lifetime.** Pause, and ask a third child to unwrap a third layer from the package. **Who can tell me if the book of Isaiah is in the Old or**

TEACHER TIP

Be sure the kids know what you mean when you say "Savior." A simple explanation would be that a Savior makes it possible for us to live forever in heaven after we die. Also explain to kids that a "testament" is a promise made. The two parts of the Bible, the Old Testament and the New Testament, are full of promises God made to his people.

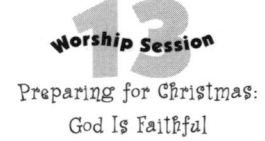

the New Testament? Allow time for kids to answer. Say: **Once again, way back in Old Testament times, God spoke to the prophet Isaiah of the Savior to come.** Read aloud Isaiah 9:6-7. Say: **All of God's people knew about the promise and waited anxiously for the Savior to come, but it took about seven hundred more years for it to happen. When the angels finally appeared to the shepherds tending their flocks on that night so many years ago and told them about the birth of Jesus, this was a sign that God had faithfully kept his promise.** Read aloud Luke 2:10-11. Ask one more child to unwrap the last layer and open the gift. Tell kids you will distribute the gifts in the box at the end of the worship session. Ask:

● **How did you feel as each layer of the package was unwrapped?**

● **Was it hard to pay attention to the story? Why or why not?**

● **How was waiting for the package to be unwrapped like the people waiting for Jesus to come?**

Say: **What you felt is anticipation. It's the excitement you feel when you know something is about to happen. People throughout the Old Testament waited in anticipation for God to keep his promise about sending Jesus.**

Waiting for the Angels

Have kids close their eyes and picture themselves on a dark hillside tending sheep as the shepherds were when the angels appeared to announce the birth of Jesus. Help children visualize what happened by asking the following questions. Say: **When I ask the following questions, try to picture in your mind what that special night was like for the shepherds.** Ask:

● **Were there any street lights?**

● **Was it very dark?**

● **Were there many stars in the sky?**

● **Do you think the shepherds were tired?**

● **What do you think they talked about as they tended their sheep?**

● **What do sheep do at night?**

● **Were the shepherds scared when the angels appeared?**

● **What did the angels look like?**

● **What do you think the shepherds felt when they realized this baby was the Savior they'd been hearing about all their lives?**

The kids will come up with all kinds of answers to these questions. Have fun speculating about those very famous shepherds and angels. After kids are given the chance to visualize the events, say: **Tell me what you saw.** Allow time for kids to respond. **Faithfulness** is the sun coming up every day and God keeping his promises.

PRAYER

Advent Reminders

Have kids each turn to a partner and tell what they know about Advent wreaths. Say: **An Advent wreath is a special decoration we use at home or at church to count down the weeks before Christmas. It helps us remember that Jesus came at Christmas. The wreath has four candles, and one is lit each Sunday as Christmas approaches until all are lit. Sometimes an extra candle is added to be lit on Christmas Day. Today we're going to make our own version of an Advent wreath. Each of you will trace and cut out four paper candles.** Give each child two pieces of purple construction paper, one piece of pink construction paper, one piece of white construction paper, a candle pattern from the "Christmas Patterns" handout (p. 103), scissors, and a pencil. Have kids trace four candles on the construction paper: three candles on the purple paper and one candle on the pink paper. Have kids cut out the candles and glue the candles to the piece of white construction paper. As kids work, ask about Christmas traditions their families follow and the special meanings those traditions have. Share a tradition from your own family, and explain why it is special to you. After kids finish gluing their candles to the sheet of construction paper, give each child a small orange flame cut from construction paper. Say: **Our candles will help remind us that Christmas is coming and God keeps his promises. Let's "light" one candle today. Glue the paper flame to one of your candles. Take your candles home with you, and on each Sunday left before Christmas, glue another flame to it or color in a flame with an orange or yellow marker.**

TEACHER TIP

If this worship session is not held on the first Sunday in Advent, light the number of candles that corresponds with the particular Sunday in Advent you are celebrating.

Promise Prayers

Say: **We've talked about promises today and how God kept a very important promise. We all make promises, and it's important to be like God and not break our promises.** Ask:

● **How does it feel when someone breaks a promise made to you?**

● **How does it feel when you break a promise you've made to another person?**

Say: **Sometimes it's hard to keep promises, but because God is faithful to his promises, we need to be faithful too.** Pray: **Thank you, God, for faithfully keeping your promises to us. Help us to serve as examples of your faithfulness when we make promises. Amen.**

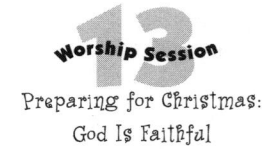

Sing the first verse of "Great Is Thy Faithfulness" again.

After the song, say: **I made a promise to you earlier that I need to keep. I said I would distribute the gifts that were in our gift package.** Distribute the gifts to the children.

TIME STRETCHERS

Advent Decorations

Provide holly leaf patterns from the "Christmas Patterns" handout (p. 103) to glue around the Advent candles kids made earlier. Give kids red and green construction paper, pencils, scissors, and glue. Instruct kids to cut out leaves and berries to add as decorations to their Advent candles.

Promise Cards

Talk with the kids about a simple promise they can make and work to keep all through the Advent season. It could be a promise to help Mom during this busy time by doing small jobs around the house, or it could be a promise to God to spend four minutes praying and reading a Bible verse. Spend some time discussing kids' promise ideas. Pass out construction paper and Christmas cookie-cutters. Have kids trace a Christmas shape and cut it out. Kids can write or draw their Advent promises on the shapes. Punch a hole in the top of the shape, and attach a loop of curling ribbon for a hanger. Have kids bring them home and hang them up—maybe on their Christmas trees—as reminders of their promises.

Christmas Patterns

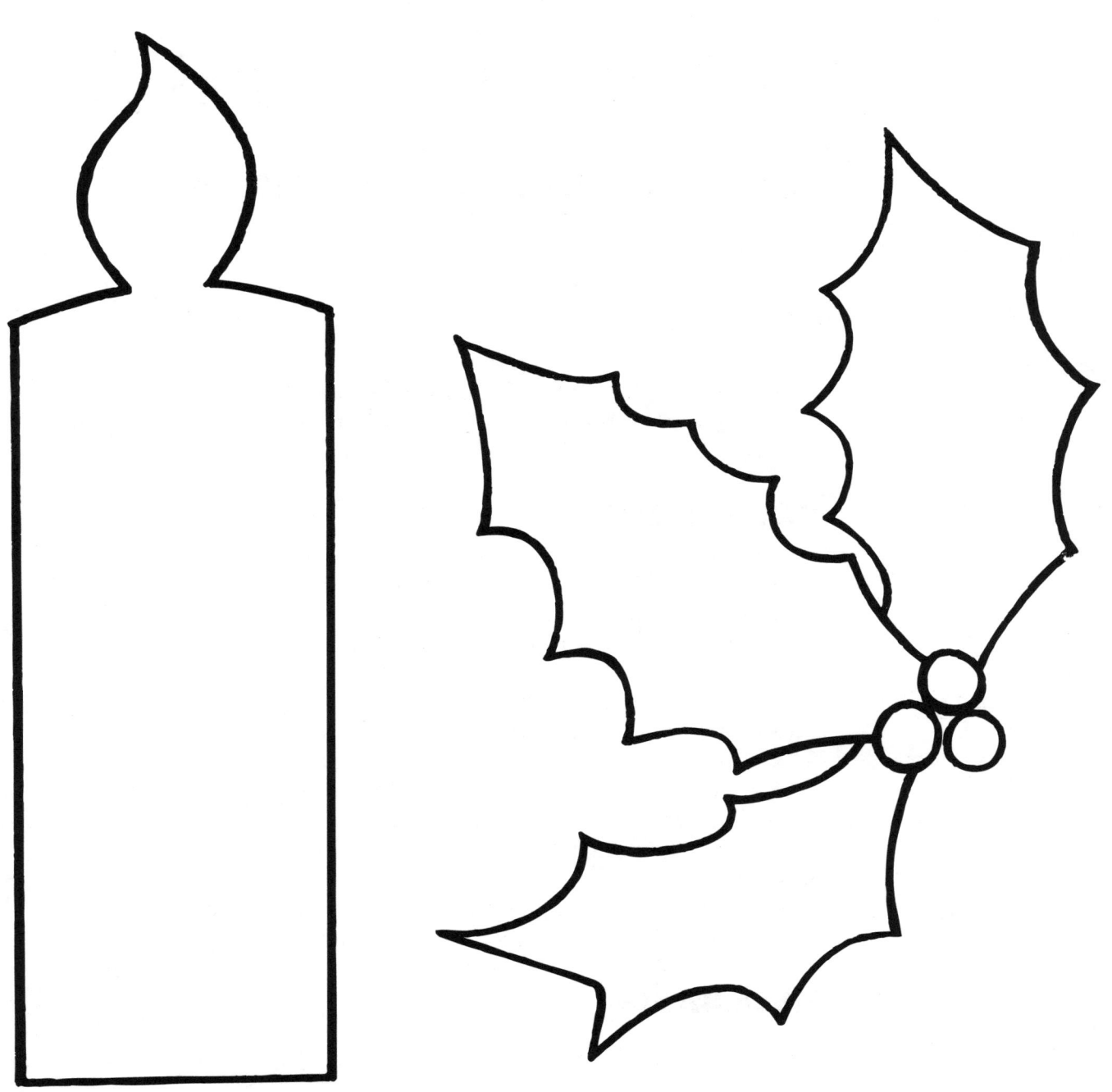

Christmas: God Saves His People

THE POINT

God became human to save us.

HOW TO USE THIS WORSHIP SESSION

Use this session during the Christmas season or any time you want to celebrate Jesus coming to live among us.

OBJECTIVES

Kids will
- celebrate the birth of Jesus, our Savior;
- discover the reason God came in human form to save us; and
- pray for those who need to put their faith in Jesus.

YOU'LL NEED

- a Bible
- baby pictures of kids in your group
- tape or glue
- poster board or a bulletin board
- a piece of soft or silky cloth
- a rose or other fragrant flower
- a picture of a fine hotel or huge castle
- a tape recording of soft music or lullabies
- a piece of rough cloth such as burlap
- a picture of a barn or stable
- a roll of Life Savers candies (regular or gummy) for every five or six children
- a lifesaving ring or inflatable pool ring (optional)
- *Group's Singable Songs for Children's Ministry* (See index on pp. 121-122.)

BIBLE BASIS

Isaiah 9:6; Matthew 1-2; and Luke 1-2

During the Christmas season, children are often reminded to "remember the real meaning of Christmas." Unfortunately, they may never actually be told what the real meaning is.

Isaiah 9:6 foretells the birth of Jesus. It told the Jewish people of long ago a Savior was coming. He would come as a child, yet he would be God.

Early portions of Matthew and Luke tell of the events surrounding the birth of Jesus. All of these details serve to remind us that God came as a baby in poor conditions just so God could let us know of his desire to rescue us from the destruction of sin.

No Christmas celebration is complete without hearing of the love of God. God's love is so great that a special baby was sent to a humble birth for the purpose of saving us from our sinfulness.

UNDERSTANDING YOUR KIDS

Christmas is probably the most popular holiday with children. And why not? Christmas means parties, singing, baking, and most of all, presents!

Because so much focus is placed on getting presents and the secular trappings of the holiday, children are sure to forget the true meaning of Christmas. Indeed, many adults have to be reminded again and again.

This worship session gives you a wonderful opportunity to share with kids the real reason we celebrate at this time of year, and to share how this relates to their young lives. This baby born so long ago is still alive and can lead us to a relationship with God. Let kids know the exciting news: Jesus came as a child so they might know God.

PRAISE

Baby Who?

Several weeks before this lesson, ask parents to send you baby pictures of the children in your group. When you've gathered enough pictures (you don't have to have one for every child), tape or lightly glue them to poster board or a bulletin board so kids can see them.

Place the picture display where children can see it as they enter the meeting area. Encourage kids to examine the board as they arrive and make guesses as to the identity of these babies.

When kids are seated, move the board to the front of the meeting area so you can refer to it. Ask children to share their guesses as to which picture belongs to which child (or adult). Then say: **We all entered this world as babies, and look at what we've already become. Our bodies have grown, our minds have learned new things, we've learned to talk. Jesus entered this world as a baby too. Even before he was born, people were talking about what he would become.**

Read aloud Isaiah 9:6, and then say: **God came as a human being, starting as a baby, to give us the gift of salvation. We don't have a picture of Jesus here, but we can praise God for sending**

TEACHER TIP

If you want to use this activity but forgot to gather pictures from parents in advance, call Sunday school teachers or other children's ministry workers and ask them for their baby pictures. The kids will get a kick out of seeing adults as they once were, you'll only have a few calls to make, and the point will still be made with just a few pictures. Be sure to include one of yourself.

105

Jesus. Offer a prayer of praise, expressing thanks to God for being willing to come to earth as a child to give the gift of salvation to the children in the group. Have kids sing "Away in a Manger" *(Group's Singable Songs for Children's Ministry).*

Fit for a King

Have children form pairs (or trios if necessary). Say: **Let's imagine that a king is going to be born and you are asked to help prepare a guest room for this baby king. What would you put in this room?** Have kids discuss their answers with their partners, and allow several children to share their answers with the whole group.

After pairs have shared, pass the soft cloth around the room for kids to feel. Say: **We might want to give a king clothes that would feel like this.** Pass around the flower for kids to smell, hold up the picture of a hotel or castle, and play the soft music on the tape recorder, asking:

● **How will flowers like this make the room smell?**
● **Is this the kind of house you'd choose for the king?**
● **How will this music make the baby and his parents feel?**

Gather the items together, and then sing "Away in a Manger" again, using motions if you like. After the song, say: **We saw a lot of nice things when we planned our guest room for a baby king. Jesus is even more important than a king. This song reminds us of what Jesus' "guest room" looked like the night he was born. How does it compare to the room we prepared for a king?** Hold up the soft cloth, and then pass around the piece of burlap or rough cloth for children to touch. Ask:

● **How do these cloths compare?**
● **Which is nicer to wrap a baby in? Why?**

Hold up the pictures of the hotel next to the picture of a barn or stable. Say: **Jesus spent his first night in a stable with animals.** Ask:

● **How does this compare to our beautiful guest room for a king?**
● **How are the smells of the stable different from the smells of the flowers we placed in the room?**
● **How are the sounds in the stable different from the sounds in our guest room?** Have children loudly do their best cow, sheep, and goat imitations.
● **How would these noises make a baby feel?**

Put away all the items you've used in the activity, and then say: **Jesus is more important than any king who ever lived. Because God loves us, Jesus came to earth as a human. He was born as a baby. And instead of a royal welcome, Jesus was wrapped in poor cloth and laid on hay in a room full of loud and smelly**

TEACHER TIP

For a large group, pass several of the same objects to the kids so all get to touch and smell the objects in a reasonable amount of time. Ask adult helpers to help you pass the objects.

animals. Ask:

● **Why do you think God wanted Jesus to come this way?**

Say: **God sent Jesus as a man to save us from sin, the bad things we do. And God knew it was best for Jesus to be treated as a very common, ordinary person instead of being hidden away and protected as royalty.** Sing "Away in a Manger" again as a reminder of how Jesus came as a human.

Before you sing the next song, say: **Jesus came as a man to rescue us and help us have a friendship with God, but he wasn't welcomed by any presidents or kings. He was welcomed by shepherds and angels. Let's pretend we're those shepherds and angels singing to Jesus all those years ago.**

Let each child decide whether he or she wants to be an angel or a shepherd. Ask all the shepherds to let you hear their shepherd voices. Let the kids decide what they should sound like. Then have the angels sound their heavenly voices. Again, let the kids determine how an angel should sound.

When all voices are ready, sing "He Is the King of Kings" *(Group's Singable Songs for Children's Ministry)*. Sing the song again, having children switch parts so each one gets a chance to be an angel and a shepherd.

POINT

Trouble at the Zoo

Choose two or three kids as volunteers. Explain that they will be "zoo keepers." Have these kids stand to the side while you give directions to the rest of the group. Say: **We need to make our meeting area into a zoo. Each of you think of an animal you can be. You can be an elephant, hyena, iguana, or any animal you want. Decide on your animal, and then show me you're ready by making the noises and actions of that animal.**

As the room begins to erupt with noise, take your zoo keepers aside and quietly explain to them that they're to deliver this message to the zoo animals: "The zoo is on fire! Follow me to safety!" Designate the front or back of the meeting area as the "safe area."

The zoo keepers can only express this message in animal words or actions. They may only speak the language of the animals.

When your zoo keepers understand their task, set them loose in the "zoo." It's likely they won't be understood by any of the "animals" and won't get anyone to follow them to safety. Even if a few animals make it to safety, they won't really know why they've followed a zoo keeper unless the volunteer slips and uses human words.

After a *short* amount of time, give your attention-getting signal, and have all animals become children again and gather together in

TEACHER TIP

For a large group of children, have kids form four equal groups. Send each group to one corner of your meeting area. Send an adult helper with each group. Have the adult helper choose the two "zoo keepers" and explain roles. Make the "safe area" one of the walls of each group's corner. Have each group participate in the activity simultaneously. You may then hold the discussion in the smaller groups or gather kids back together in the larger group.

a large group. Ask:

● **What did you think the zoo keepers were doing as they rushed about the meeting area?**

● **Did any of you follow them? Why or why not?**

● **How were they trying to communicate with you?**

Ask the zoo keepers to share in human language what they attempted to communicate. Then say: **These zoo keepers knew there was a fire in the zoo. They wanted you to move to safety. If this had happened in real life, how would the zoo keepers have let the animals know there was danger?** Allow kids time to answer. Then say: **If this was a real zoo, the zoo keepers would move the animals to safety, but the animals would never understand why they'd been moved. What's the only true way we can communicate our message to animals?** Allow kids time to answer. **We'd have to become animals ourselves so we could use true animal communication.**

Ask:

● **How is this game similar to what Jesus did, coming as a human?**

● **How are we similar to the animals in the zoo?**

● **How is Jesus like the zoo keeper?**

Say: **We live in a world that keeps us away from God, and there is the danger that we'll never know God. God became a human so that we can know God. Jesus came to earth to tell us in our language that God loves us and wants to rescue us from sin. The best way for God to save us was to become one of us.**

The First Christmas

Say: **Sometimes when Christmas comes, we forget why we're celebrating. It's because Jesus came to earth as our Savior. Let's read the story of the very first Christmas to help us remember why we celebrate this special holiday.** Before you tell the Christmas story, prepare children to participate in the following ways:

● Kids wearing mostly white should say "baa" every time you say the words "shepherd" or "sheep."

● Kids wearing mostly yellow, gold, or orange should sing out "hallelujah" every time you say the words "angel" or "angels."

● Kids wearing mostly blue or green should cradle their arms and whisper "shh" every time you say the word "baby."

● Kids wearing mostly red or purple should scratch their heads and murmur "hmm" every time the wise men are mentioned.

● Kids wearing more than one color can participate in more than one action.

When everyone understands his or her part, tell the following story:

TEACHER TIP

One child is sure to point out that humans can communicate with primates through hand signals or dolphins through whistles. If so, use this as a discussion starter and make the point that God has communicated with us in basic ways such as through creation (Psalm 97:6) and through our own consciences (Romans 2:14-16). However, the best way for God to communicate with humans was to become human.

In Matthew 1-2 and Luke 1-2, the Bible tells us about how Jesus was born.

God sent an *angel* named Gabriel to the home of a young woman named Mary. Gabriel the *angel* told Mary not to be afraid because God was pleased with her and wanted her to be the mother of a *baby* she should name Jesus. Jesus would be God's Son.

Mary was engaged to be married to a man named Joseph. God also sent an *angel* to visit Joseph. The *angel* told Joseph not to be afraid, too, and that Mary would have a *baby* they should name Jesus. This *baby* would be God's Son, and he would save people from their sins.

Several months later, the emperor wanted to count all the people in the land. He made a law that everyone had to return to the town of their family to register and be counted. Joseph and Mary traveled to Bethlehem because that was where Joseph's family was from.

When Mary and Joseph arrived in Bethlehem, there was no room for them in the inn, so they stayed in a stable. The time came for the *baby* to be born, and when Mary gave birth to *baby* Jesus, she wrapped him in cloths and placed him in a manger.

In the fields nearby, there were *shepherds* watching over their *sheep* that night. Suddenly an *angel* of the Lord appeared to them, and God's glory shone all around them. The *shepherds* were terrified! But the *angel* said, "Do not be afraid. I bring you good news of great joy that will be for all the people. Today in the town of David a Savior has been born to you; he is Christ the Lord." The *angel* told the *shepherds* where they could find the *baby*, and then the *angel* was joined by many more *angels*, who praised God for sending Jesus to save all people.

The *shepherds* hurried off and found Mary and Joseph and the *baby*. They told others about what they had seen and heard. Some time later, a group of *wise men* who studied the stars noticed a special star in the east and believed it meant a new king had been born. The *wise men* followed this star and came to the house where Jesus then lived. The *wise men* gave him presents of gold, incense, and myrrh, which is an expensive spice.

Jesus grew into a boy and then a man. This is how Jesus came to live on the earth as a man, sent to save us from sin.

PRAYER

Lifesavers

Have kids form groups of five or six and sit together in a circle. Give one child in each group a roll of Life Savers candies. Have the

child hold the candy without opening it. If you have a lifesaving ring or inflatable pool ring, hold this up now. Ask:

● **What is a lifesaver for?**

● **How does it save a person's life?**

Say: **The Life Savers you have are candy. They remind us that Jesus came to earth as a man to be our Savior. If we believe that Jesus is God's Son and that Jesus died on the cross and came back to life, we can be forgiven of all the wrong things we do and be saved from life without God.**

Let's use these Life Savers candies to help us pray. If you're holding the roll of candy, open it now and give each person in your circle one Life Savers candy. When each child has a Life Savers candy, say: **Before you eat your candy, take turns praying in your circle. You can thank God for coming to earth as a human to be our Savior. You can thank God for all Jesus did to save us. Or you can pray for someone who doesn't know about Jesus.**

Let children pray in their circles. If you have time and enough candies, give each child a second Life Savers candy, and let kids pray around the circle again.

Pray aloud for those who don't know about Jesus, and pray that those gathered in the room will look for ways to share this important message with others.

TIME STRETCHER

Cookie Twins

Prepare by baking or purchasing gingerbread cookies. You'll need enough so that each child can have one. You'll also need tubes of frosting in a variety of colors. If you like, you can use decorative candies and sprinkles as well. Have wet cloths handy for sticky fingers. Place tables around the meeting area with cookies and decorating supplies on each table.

Say: **I'm going to give each of you the chance to decorate a cookie to look just like you. There are gingerbread cookies and frosting on the tables. Take one cookie, and use the frosting to make it look as much like you as possible. Can you match its hair color to yours? Give it your color of eyes? Frost on clothes that look like yours? Get started!**

After children frost their cookies, have them return to their seats. Have them show you their cookies. Compare their cookies to how the children actually look. Ask:

● **Could we decorate a cookie to look exactly like us?**

● **Would any amount of decorating ever make one of these cookies into a real person? Why not?**

These cookies can remind us about Jesus becoming a human

TEACHER TIP

If you don't have the time or budget for gingerbread cookies, substitute paper cut-outs in the shape of gingerbread people.

to save us. God didn't just make himself look like us, as we make these cookies look like us. God became one of us to save us from sin. Allow children to eat their cookie "twins."

Christmas: God Is Peace

God sent Jesus to mend our relationships with God and each other.

HOW TO USE THIS WORSHIP SESSION

Use this session during the Christmas season or any time you want your kids to reflect on God's peace.

OBJECTIVES

Kids will
● discover what it means to be at peace with others,
● learn that God sent Jesus so we could be at peace with God, and
● discover ways they can incorporate God's peace into their own lives and relationships.

YOU'LL NEED

● Bibles
● white drawing or construction paper
● colorful markers
● a birth announcement
● colored construction paper
● 8½x11-inch white paper
● colored paper scraps
● glue
● a stapler
● 8½x11-inch red card stock, cut into fourths
● candy canes

BIBLE BASIS

Luke 2:8-14

The angels surprised the unsuspecting shepherds with words from God about a promised Savior who came to bring peace on earth. When we think about peace on earth today, our thoughts turn to the areas of the world where people turn against people, the places where violence and death are everyday occurrences. But the angels talked about something a bit more personal. They heralded

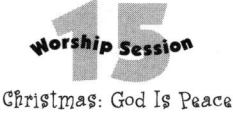

the coming of One who brings about humanity's reconciliation with God. When peace is reestablished in that relationship, then only can peace be established between human beings.

Pictures and images of Christmas show it to be a peaceful holiday, but sometimes it's anything but. Much of the Christmas season is stressful, and it can be a time when our relationships with others fray. How appropriate, then, to turn our eyes to the coming of the Prince of Peace. Christmas is a time not only to reflect on our relationship with God, but also to reflect on our relationships with others.

UNDERSTANDING YOUR KIDS

Fighting with other kids and siblings is part of childhood. Kids don't always lead the most peaceful existence. Relational skills need to be taught and practiced. We want to teach kids that the goal in relationships is peace, not war.

But kids need a relationship with God, too. They need reconciliation with God and to enjoy harmony in their relationship with him. When that is established, they will desire harmony in their relationships with others.

Use this Christmas season to talk with your kids about the coming of Jesus, who made peace between God and people by giving his life. Talk with kids about their relationship with God and about how that relationship can help them live peacefully with others.

PRAISE

Discovering Peace

Have kids form groups of three or four. If you have a smaller group, have each child find a partner. Make sure you have kids who can read and write in groups with kids who can not yet read and write. Give each group white construction paper or drawing paper and various colors of markers. Assign each member of the group a job. One of the group members will be the recorder, who will write the group's ideas on paper. Another member will be the reporter, who will tell the whole class the group's findings. If there's another member of each group, let that child be the peacemaker, who keeps the peace if there's a disagreement of ideas. If your groups have four members, have the fourth child be the encourager, who helps everyone participate. Say: **In your groups, write the word "peace" on your paper. Then try and think of as many words as you can that describe what peace is—but the words can only begin with the letters in the word peace. For example, you might use the word "patient" because peace begins with the letter "p," or "easy" because the letter "e" is found in the word peace.** Give groups five

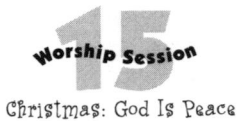

to ten minutes to work on their answers. Bring the kids back together in a large group, and have them share their words describing peace. Ask:

● **Was it hard or easy to think of words that describe peace? Why?**

● **What are some places where it's important to have peace?**

● **What are some ways we can make our lives peaceful?**

Say: **It's important to have peace and harmony in our relationships with God and with other people. God knew that it was good for us to live in peace with each other. So Jesus was born at Christmas to bring peace to everyone on earth.**

That Sounds Awful

Have each child find a partner. Say: **When I say "go," I want you to tell your partner what you look forward to about Christmas. Don't wait for one person to talk before you talk. I want you all to talk at the same time. Go!** Let kids talk long enough so the noise fills the room. Then use an attention-getting signal to bring kids' attention back to you. Ask:

● **What did your partner say about Christmas?**

● **Was it hard to hear to your partner? Why?**

● **How did you feel as you tried to understand what your partner said?**

Say: **Turn to your partner again, and tell him or her what you are looking forward to about Christmas. But this time speak one at a time.** When kids are done sharing, ask:

● **What made it easier to listen to your partner this time?**

Say: **The first time you talked about Christmas with your partners, it was hard to hear what they said. It was hard to listen to them because everyone was talking at once. It wasn't very peaceful. But the second time you talked to your partners, it was easier to hear and understand because some people were listening. Not everyone talked at once. It was more peaceful. When we don't have peace in our relationships with God and others, sometimes it's hard to understand them. Now let's look at another way to define peace.** Ask the group:

● **How many of you take music lessons? What instruments do you play?** Allow kids time to respond.

● **For those of you who don't take music lessons, who do you know that plays some kind of musical instrument, and what instrument is it?**

● **When you or someone you know plays a musical instrument and plays the correct notes, how does it sound?**

Say: **When the music sounds good to our ears, that's called harmony. But how does it sound when they play the wrong**

notes? When music doesn't sound good to our ears, we know the music is not in harmony. Relationships with God and others are like that too. When we have peace with God and our friends, it makes a good sound, or harmony, in God's ears. But when we're not at peace with God and each other, then it's like playing the wrong notes in a song.

Angelic Announcement

Lead kids in singing verses 1 and 3 of the familiar Christmas carol "Hark! the Herald Angels Sing." Make sure you explain any words kids may not understand. For example, "herald" is used to describe someone bringing an important message, and "hark" is a signal to listen carefully. After you finish singing, say: **This Christmas carol tells us about the announcement the angels made to the shepherds when Jesus was born. Let's talk more about what the angels said.**

Have kids get back into their groups from the first activity. Give each group a Bible. Have groups look up and read Luke 2:8-14. After they read the passage, have them discuss the following questions in their groups:

● **What is the good news the angels told the shepherds?**

● **Who is the good news for?**

● **What gift does God want to give to all the people on earth through Jesus?**

● **Do you think all the people on earth have accepted this gift of peace? Why?**

● **What would happen if they did? What would our world look like?**

Gather kids back together in the large group, and say: **God sent the angels to tell the shepherds Jesus had been born. They praised God for sending someone who would bring peace to all the people on earth. God sent Jesus to be born so all people on earth could have peace with God and each other. But some people don't want to be at peace with God and each other. They don't want to accept the gift. But even so, Jesus brought the gift of peace and cares about people more than anything else.**

Hold up a birth announcement. Say: **Instead of sending a card in the mail to announce Jesus' birth, God sent a group of angels. They came to announce Jesus' birth to the shepherds. Because of Jesus' birth, we can have peace with God.**

Peacemaking Prayers

Lead kids in a time of prayer, encouraging them to think of situations in their lives in which they need Jesus' help to bring the gift

TEACHER TIP

If you have a piano or other musical instrument available in your meeting area, play the notes for a C chord to illustrate harmony. Then play a group of notes together at random to illustrate disharmony.

Worship Session 15

Christmas: God Is Peace

TEACHER TIP

Find someone who can accompany the singing, or record an accompaniment before class. Or ask a child with musical ability to accompany the class. Ask the child the week before this worship session. We send a powerful message to kids when we allow them to use their talents in the worship of God.

of peace. Allow those who wish to share to give one-sentence examples of where they need the peace of Jesus. After each child who wants to has shared his or her prayer request, pray for those children. At the end of the prayer, have the whole group say, **"Thank you, God, for sending Jesus to bring us peace."**

Lead kids in singing verses 1 and 3 of "Hark! the Herald Angels Sing" again.

POINT

Peace Journal

Have the kids make a peace journal. Give each child a piece of colored construction paper, several sheets of 8½x11-inch white writing paper, markers, colored paper scraps, glue, and any other art supplies you want to use. Say: **Because Jesus came to bring peace, people who know God can have this peace both with God and with other people. We'll use these art supplies to make a peace journal. A journal is a place to write or draw our feelings, and in this journal we'll write or draw about our disagreements with others. Sometimes writing or drawing our thoughts first helps us to use peaceful words when we talk to the person we're fighting with. Writing or drawing in our journals can help us find peaceful ways to solve problems.** Have kids fold the piece of construction paper in half to make the journal cover. Using the markers, colored paper scraps, and other art supplies, have kids decorate the cover of their journals. After they finish decorating the covers, have kids take several sheets of the writing paper, fold them in half, and insert them into the folded construction paper to make a book. You may staple the sides of the book to keep the paper inside. Say: **Now think of a situation you might write or draw about in this book. Think of a situation that needs to be more peaceful. Maybe you had a fight with your brother, or maybe some kids at school are hard to get along with. Write or draw about that situation in your journal.**

Give kids time to work in their journals. When kids finish with this, say: **Think about how Jesus can help you in this situation. What do you think Jesus would do in this situation? Maybe you need to ask for Jesus' help to bring peace. Maybe you know Jesus wants you to apologize for something you did. Continue to work in your journals. Draw or write what you can do to make this situation more peaceful with Jesus' help.**

After kids finish, gather them back together in a large group, and ask:

● **How can using your journals to think about peaceful relationships help you give peace to others?**

POINT

Encourage kids to take their journals home and add to them during the week. Ask them to think about how they can make the situations they encounter at home and at school more peaceful with Jesus' help.

PRAYER

Giving Peace

Have kids think about someone they know and care about who they may not be at peace with or who might need a more peaceful life. It could be the same situation they worked with in their journals. Give kids an example such as a disagreement with a sister over whose turn it is to set the table for dinner. Say: **To begin the process of giving peace, we need Jesus' help. Let's make gift tags to let others know that Jesus came to bring the gift of peace.** Give each child a piece of the red card stock and a marker. Have kids write the words "Jesus Brings _____ Peace" on the card stock. Have the kids who are able to write help the younger ones. Say: **Now think of someone who needs a more peaceful life, someone you might give a gift to. Write that person's name in the blank space.** After kids complete their gift tags, invite the group to sit in a circle on the floor. Ask kids to silently pray for either the person whose name they wrote on the tag or for the situation they worked with in their journals. End the prayer time by asking God to bring peace into all the situations the kids prayed for.

Encourage kids to use the peace gift tag during the next week or for Christmas gift-giving. Or use the tags in conjunction with the next activity, suggesting that kids give a candy cane as a gift.

Candy Cane Reminders

Hand each child a red and white candy cane. Say: **The candy cane can be more than something sweet we get at Christmas-time. It can be a reminder of the story of how Jesus was born at Christmas and how he came to bring us peace with God and with each other. See how it's shaped like a shepherd's crook? This helps us to remember the shepherds who heard the words from the angels about Jesus coming to bring peace to all people. So this Christmas whenever you see a candy cane, remember that Jesus came to help us have peaceful relationships with God and each other.**

Close the session in prayer, once again thanking God for being a God of peace and asking help in developing peaceful relationships.

TEACHER TIP

For a very large group, ask kids to form several prayer circles. Ask an adult helper to sit with each circle.

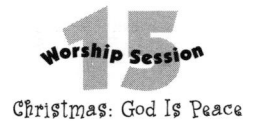

TIME STRETCHER

Peace Banner

Before the worship session, obtain one or two yards of lightly colored cloth. Make a banner by folding over the edges and using fusible webbing to seal the edges. You can find fusible webbing in fabric stores. It's generally used to hem a garment without actually sewing it. Use the ½-inch size used for hemming garments. Seal the edges of the banner using a hot iron with the steam switch turned on.

During the worship session, have one child write the words "Jesus Is Our Prince of Peace" with a dark purple marker on the banner. Then involve everyone in making the banner. Have kids decorate the edges with other markers and art supplies you have available. If you have a large class, make two banners. Hang the banner in a hallway of your church so others will learn with your class.

To simplify this project, use large sheets of newsprint or butcher paper to make the banners.

Indexes

Scripture Index

Group's Singable Songs for Children's Ministry Index

When you use songs from *Group's Singable Songs for Children's Ministry*, this index will help you locate the songs. For each song, we've listed where you'll find it in the accompaniment and leaders guide, on which volume of cassette or CD you'll find the song, and whether the song is included in a Lyrics Big Book.

SESSION 1: God Is All-Knowing

"This Is the Day"

Accompaniment and Leaders Guide: p. 97
Cassette or CD: volume 3
Lyrics Big Book for More Group Singing

SESSION 2: God Is Loving

"Lord, I Lift Your Name on High"

Accompaniment and Leaders Guide: p. 10
Cassette or CD: volume 1
Lyrics Big Book for Group Singing

"His Banner Over Me Is Love"

Accompaniment and Leaders Guide: p. 92
Cassette or CD: volume 2
Lyrics Big Book for Group Singing

SESSION 3: God Is Forgiving

"Sing (If You Wanna Be Happy)"

Accompaniment and Leaders Guide: p. 147
Cassette or CD: volume 4
Lyrics Big Book for More Group Singing

"He Forgives Me"

Accompaniment and Leaders Guide: p. 43
Cassette or CD: volume 1
Lyrics Big Book for Group Singing

Session 4: God Is Creator

"The Butterfly Song"

Accompaniment and Leaders Guide: p. 98
Cassette or CD: volume 3
Lyrics Big Book for More Group Singing

"Psalm 139:14"

Accompaniment and Leaders Guide: p. 125
Cassette or CD: volume 3

SESSION 5: God Is Rest

"This Is the Day"

Accompaniment and Leaders Guide: p. 97
Cassette or CD: volume 3
Lyrics Big Book for More Group Singing

"Seek Ye First"

Accompaniment and Leaders Guide: p. 157
Cassette or CD: volume 4

SESSION 6: God Provides for All Our Needs

"Everybody Give Thanks!"

Accompaniment and Leaders Guide: p. 38
Cassette or CD: volume 1
Lyrics Big Book for Group Singing

"Rejoice in the Lord Always"

Accompaniment and Leaders Guide: p. 138
Cassette or CD: volume 3

SESSION 8: God Is Joyful

"Down in My Heart"

Accompaniment and Leaders Guide: p. 46
Cassette or CD: volume 1

"Ha-La-La-La"

Accompaniment and Leaders Guide: p. 95
Cassette or CD: volume 3
Lyrics Big Book for More Group Singing

Session 9: God Is Good

"What a Mighty God We Serve"

Accompaniment and Leaders Guide: p. 159
Cassette or CD: volume 4

"God's Not Dead"

Accompaniment and Leaders Guide: p. 66
Cassette or CD: volume 2

Session 10: Palm Sunday: God Is Our King

"King of Kings"

Accompaniment and Leaders Guide: p. 115
Cassette or CD: volume 3

Session 11: Easter: God Is Forever

"Ho-Ho-Ho-Hosanna"

Accompaniment and Leaders Guide: p. 89
Cassette or CD: volume 2
Lyrics Big Book for Group Singing

"He's Alive"

Accompaniment and Leaders Guide: p. 55
Cassette or CD: volume 2

Session 12: Easter: God Is All-Powerful

"God's Not Dead"

Accompaniment and Leaders Guide: p. 66
Cassette or CD: volume 2

"He's Alive"

Accompaniment and Leaders Guide: p. 55
Cassette or CD: volume 2

"Awesome God"

Accompaniment and Leaders Guide: p. 19
Cassette or CD: volume 1

Session 14: Christmas: God Saves His People

"Away in a Manger"

Accompaniment and Leaders Guide: p. 31
Cassette or CD: volume 1

"He Is the King of Kings"

Accompaniment and Leaders Guide: p. 91
Cassette or CD: volume 2

Bible Story Index

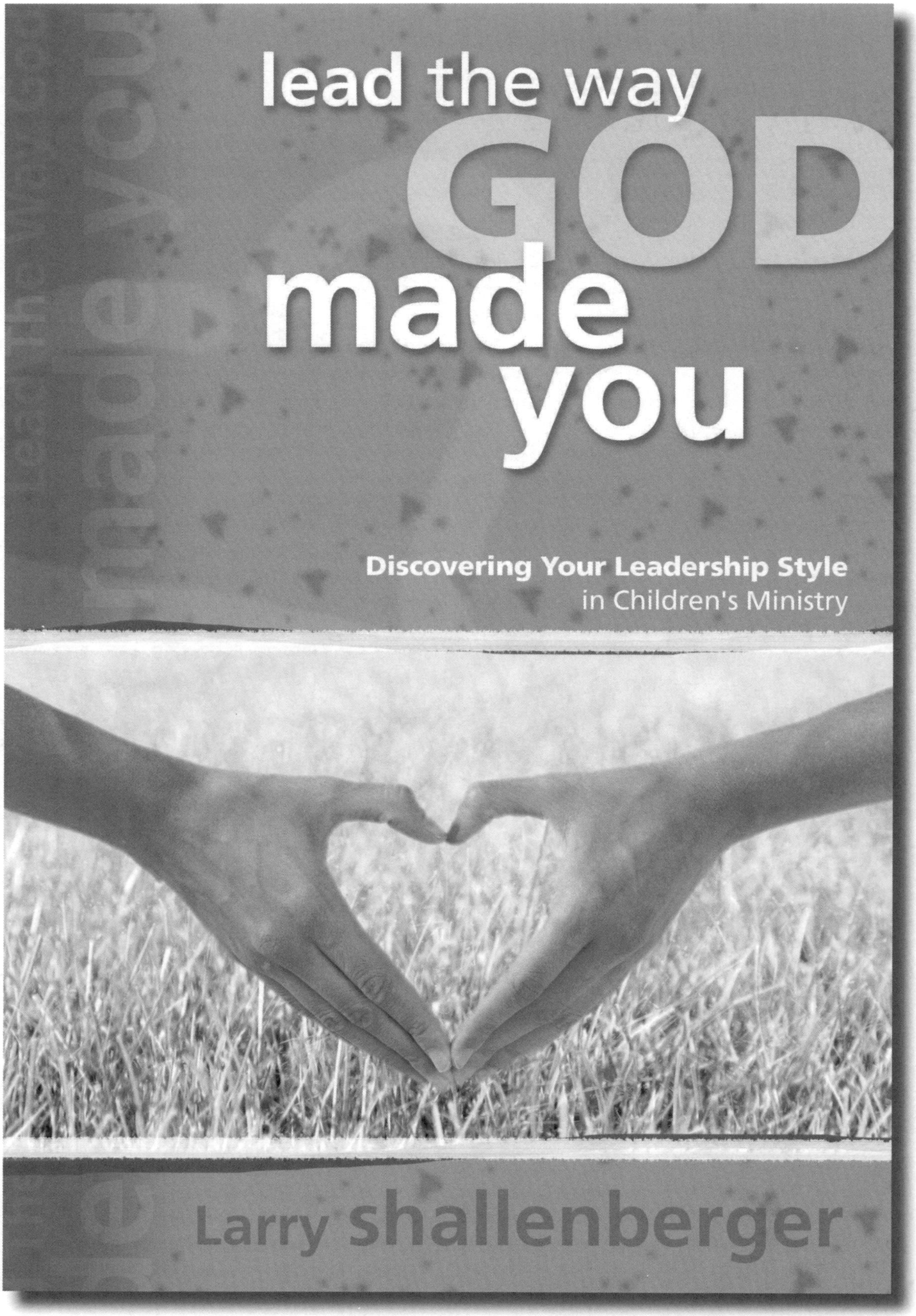
lead the way
GOD
made
you
Discovering Your Leadership Style
in Children's Ministry
Larry shallenberger

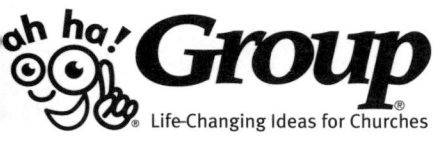

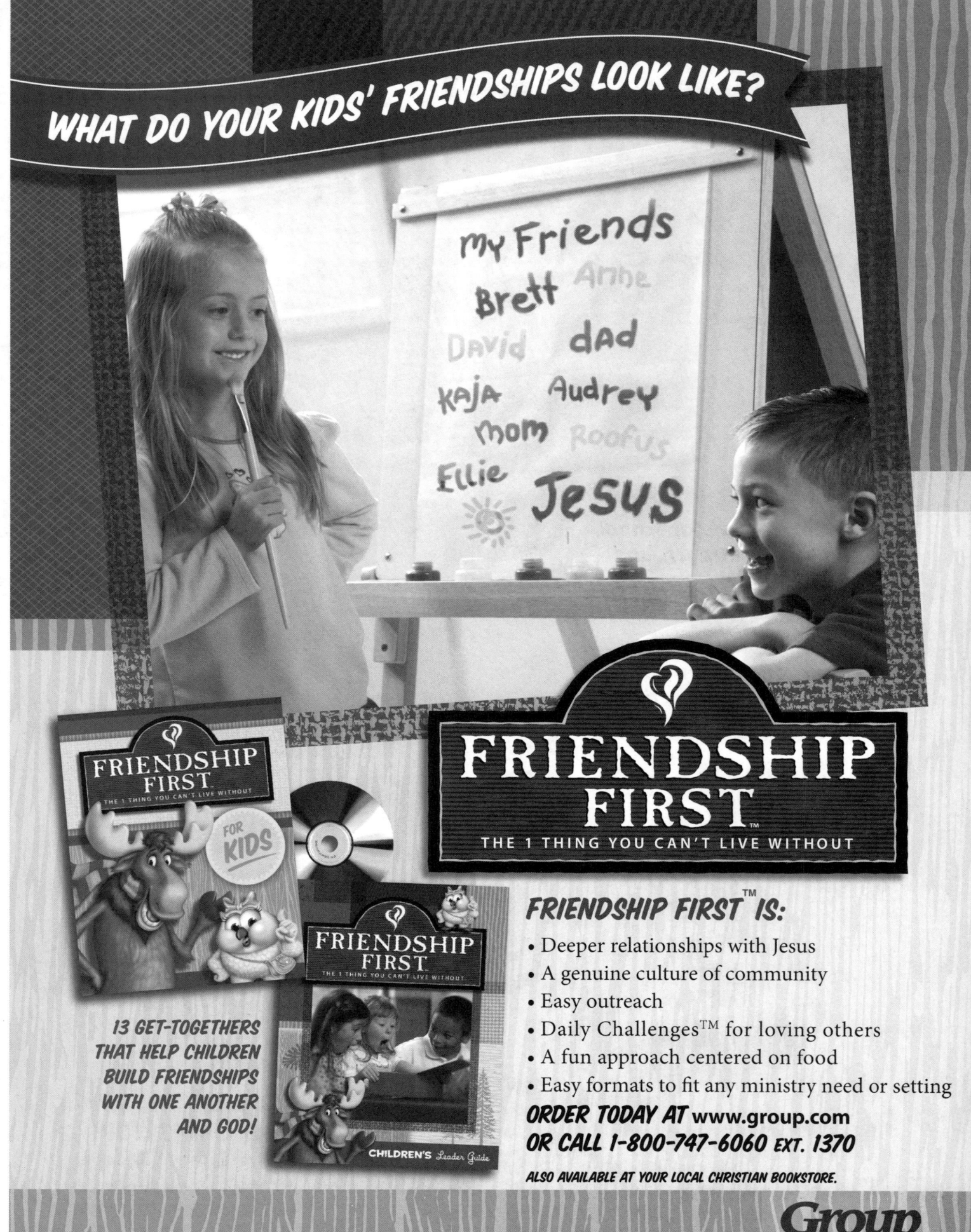